Women of the Ocean State:

25 Rhode Island Women You Should Know

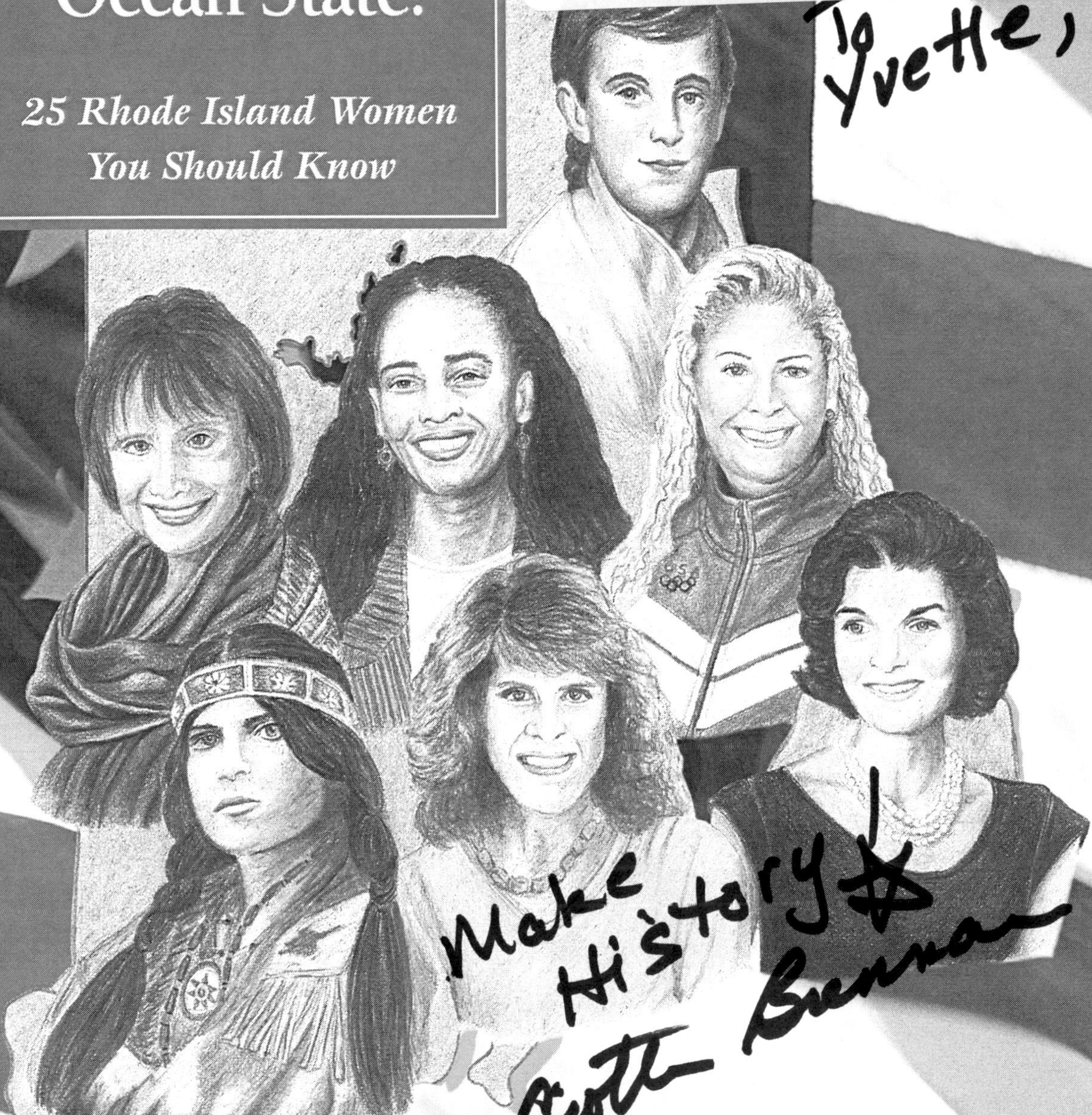

Written by Linda Crotta Brennan and Others • Illustrated by Lisa Greenleaf

***Apprentice Shop Books,* LLC**
Amherst, New Hampshire

For information regarding permissions contact:
Apprentice Shop Books, LLC
P.O. Box 375
Amherst, NH 03031
www.apprenticeshopbooks.com

LIBRARY OF CONGRESS CATALOGING-IN-PUBLICATION DATA

Brennan, Linda Crotta

Women of the Ocean State: 25 Rhode Island Women You Should Know by Linda Crotta Brennan and Others. Illustrations copyright © 2013 by Lisa Greenleaf

Summary: Profiles of 25 influential Rhode Island women. Includes bibliographies for additional research.

1. Rhode Island, Juvenile non-fiction. 2. Famous Rhode Island women. 3. Women artists—United States—Rhode Island—biography—juvenile literature. 4. Women athletes—United States—Rhode Island —biography—juvenile literature. 5. Women writers—United States—Rhode Island—biography—juvenile literature. 6. Women in public service—United States—Rhode Island—biography—juvenile literature. 7. Women scientists—United States— Rhode Island—biography—juvenile literature.

ISBN-13: 978-0-9842549-7-2
ISBN-10: 0-9842549-7-8

Printed in United States of America

On the cover: Clockwise from the bottom right: Jacqueline Kennedy Onassis, Ruth Buzzi, Princess Redwing, Claudine Schneider, O. Rogeriee Thompson, Prudence Crandall, Elizabeth Beisel

Cover design, illustrations, and book design by Lisa Greenleaf
Greenleaf Design Studio *www.Lisagreenleaf.com*

A Timeline of Rhode Island History

1636 ➢ Roger Williams founds Providence Plantations Colony. It will join the colony of Rhode Island in 1644.

1637 ➢ **Anne Hutchinson** stands trial for blasphemy against the Puritan religion.

1736 ➢ Widow **Ann Smith Franklin** becomes the official printer to the colony of Rhode Island.

1776 ➢ Rhode Island becomes the first American colony to declare independence from British rule.

1790 ➢ Rhode Island, the last American colony to ratify the US Constitution, becomes a state.

1833 ➢ **Prudence Crandall** defies Rhode Island's new "Black Law" and continues to educate young women of color. Violence against the school and its students will force its closure in 1834.

c1835 ➢ The home of **Elizabeth Buffum Chace** becomes a stop on the Underground Railroad.

1838 ➢ **Frances Harriet Whipple Green McDougall** anonymously publishes *The Memoirs of Elleanor Eldridge*, a true story about the life of a free black woman.

1855 ➢ **Christiana Carteaux Bannister**, an African American businesswoman, opens a hair salon in Providence.

1861 ➢ **Julia Ward Howe** pens *The Battle Hymn of the Republic,* one of the Union's most popular Civil War songs.

1866 ➢ Rhode Island abolishes racial segregation in public schools.

1891 ➢ Thanks to **Sarah Elizabeth Doyle**, women are admitted to Brown University.

1892 ➢ **Matilda Sissieretta Joyner Jones** sings for President Benjamin Harrison at the White House.

1895 ➢ **Annie Smith Peck** captures world attention by climbing the Matterhorn.

1911 ➢ On the night of her death, ships' bells toll throughout Newport Harbor for lighthouse keeper **Ida Lewis**, "The Bravest Woman in America".

1912 ➢ **Alva Vanderbilt Belmont** leads Political Equality League members in New York City's Women's Votes Parade.

1922 ➢ After facing racial prejudice, **Nancy Elizabeth Prophet** moves to Paris to study sculpture.

1952 ➢ **Janet Moreau** earns gold in the Women's Relay at the Summer Olympics in Helsinki, Finland.

1958 ➢ **Princess Red Wing** and Eva Lutz Butler open the Tomaquag Indian Memorial Museum.

1965 ➢ Astrologer and actor **Joyce Jillson** wins the Theatre World award for her Broadway performance in *The Roar of the Greasepaint – the Smell of the Crowd.*

1973 ➢ The television comedy hit *Laugh In* ends its run; **Ruth Buzzi** performed in all 140 episodes.

1975 ➢ Former first lady **Jacqueline Kennedy Onassis** takes a job as book editor at Viking Press.

1980 ➢ **Claudine Schneider** becomes the first woman to represent Rhode Island when she is elected to Congress.

1993 ➢ When the Dept. of Defense changes its policy, **Martha McSally** becomes one of the first women to command a fighter squadron.

1997 ➢ **Jennifer Murray** becomes the first female helicopter pilot to fly around the world.

2005 ➢ Tennis ace **Jill Craybas** defeats Serena Williams at Wimbledon.

2008 ➢ **Elizabeth Beisel** becomes the youngest member of the US Olympic Swim Team in Beijing, China.

2009 ➢ **Ojetta Rogeriee Thompson** is appointed to the US Court of Appeals for the First Circuit.

Author Credits

"Ann Smith Franklin: Colonial Printer," "Prudence Crandall: Fighter for Equal Rights to Education," "Frances Harriet Whipple Green McDougall: Writer for Those in Need," "Princess Red Wing: Speaker for her Tribe," "Claudine Schneider: Congresswoman and Environmental Leader" © 2013 Linda Crotta Brennan

"Annie Smith Peck: Mountain Climber" © 2013 by Deborah Bruss

"Jacqueline Kennedy Onassis: First Lady of the United States" © 2013 by Tammy Gagne

"Nancy Elizabeth Prophet: African-American Sculptor" © 2013 by K. D. Huxman

"Jennifer Murray: Record Breaking Helicopter Pilot" © 2013 by Cheryl Mansfield

"Elizabeth Beisel: Olympic Swimmer" © 2013 by Marcia Maynard"

"Christiana Carteaux Bannister: Black Businesswoman and Community Activist," "Sarah Elizabeth Doyle: Champion for Women's Education," "O. Rogeriee Thompson: A Judge for Changing Times" © 2013 by Cheryl Kirk Noll

"Joyce Jillson: Actress, Author, Astrologer," "Jill Craybas: Tennis Star, Olympic Athlete" © 2013 Barbara Keevil Parker

"Julia Ward Howe: Poet and Reformer" © 2013 by Jo Pitkin

"Anne Hutchinson: Co-founder of Rhode Island, Religious Activist," "Ida Lewis: Lighthouse Keeper, American Heroine" © 2013 by Sally Riley

"Janet Moreau Stone: Olympic Gold Medal Runner," "Ruth Buzzi: Actor and Comedian" © 2013 by Laurie Toupin

"Elizabeth Buffum Chace: Activist and Reformer," "Matilda Sissieretta Joyner Jones: Opera Singer" © 2013 by Barbara Turner

"Elleanor Eldridge: Laborer and Business Woman" © 2013 by Sally Wilkins

"Martha McSally: Warrior Pilot" © 2013 by Tabatha Yeatts

Photo and Illustration Credits

Cover and pages 7, 12, 27, and 39: illustrated by Lisa Greenleaf

Page 9 Courtesy of Wikipedia Commons

Page 14 Newport Historical Society & Miriam Y. Holden Collection. Rare Books Division. Department of Rare Books and Special Collections. Princeton University Library

Pages 17 & 19 Frances H. Green and Elleanor Eldridge. Memoirs of Elleanor Eldridge. Providence, R. I.: B.T. Albro, 1838

Page 22 Division of Rare and Manuscript Collections, Cornell University Library

Page 24 Connect Kids/State of Connecticut

Page 29 Green, Frances. Analytical class-book of botany, designed for academies and private students. In two parts: Part 1. Elements of vegetable structure and physiology. New York: D. Appleton, 1805-1878

Page 32 Blackstone River Valley National Heritage/ National Park Service

Page 34 Siebert, Wilbur H. The Underground Railroad from Slavery to Freedom. New York: The MacMillan Company, 1898

Page 37 Edward M. Bannister, American, 1828 – 1901

Portrait of Madame Christiana Corteaux Bannister Oil on canvas, 36" x 28 ¼"Newport Art Museum, by extended loan of the Rhode Island Black Heritage Society in trust of Bannister House

Page 42 Courtesy of Library of Congress

Page 44 Courtesy of Library of Congress

Page 47 Brown University

Page 49 Courtesy of Library of Congress

Page 52 Courtesy of Wikipedia Commons

Page 54 The Mariners' Museum, Newport News, VA

Page 57 & 59 Courtesy of Library of Congress

Page 62 Courtesy of Wikipedia Commons

Page 64 Women of Protest: Photographs from the Records of the National Woman's Party, Manuscript Division, Library of Congress, Washington, D.C.

Page 67 Haley, James T. Sparkling Gems of Race Knowledge Worth Reading.Nashville, TN: J.T. Haley & Co., 1897

Page 69 Courtesy of Library of Congress

Page 72 Nancy Elizabeth Prophet Collection, James P. Adams Library, Rhode Island College

Page 74 National Archives

Page 77 Courtesy of Sally Wilkins

Page 79 Apprentice Shop Books

Page 82 Courtesy of Wikipedia Commons

Page 84 © Bettmann/CORBIS

Pages 87 & 89 Courtesy of Library of Congress

Pages 92 & 94 Apprentice Shop Books

Page 97 ©Reuters/CORBIS

Page 99 Courtesy of Smithsonian Air and Space Museum

Page 102 Ron Moody/Findagrave.com

Page 104 Courtesy of Bowtie Press

Page 107 Courtesy of Wikipedia Commons

Page 109 Courtesy of Wikipedia Commons

Page 112 Courtesy of Wikipedia Commons

Page 114 Courtesy of Mayor Cicilline's Office

Pages 117 & 119 Courtesy of U.S. Air Force

Page 122 Courtesy of Jill Craybas

Page 124 ©2012 Mai Techaphan / Shutterstock.com

Page 127 Courtesy of USA Swimming.com

Page 129 AP Photo/Mark J. Terrill

Table of Contents

— 1 —

Anne Hutchinson: Co-founder of Rhode Island, Religious Activist

by Sally P. Riley

Anne held her baby daughter close. Her ten other children huddled between her and their father. The wind was strong and ocean waves crashed. The Hutchinson family was sailing to America on a small ship called the *Griffin*. They had left their home in England almost two months earlier. They were crowded into a space below the wooden deck. It was cold and dark and damp from seawater. Only a week ago, the weather had been sunny and terribly hot.

Nearly 100 people, 100 cows, and some pigs were on the *Griffin*. The passengers had little food and no way to keep the food cool and safe to eat.

Anne comforted her family by telling them God had revealed to her that they would land on September 18th. They did land on that date. But three years later, God's **revelation** would cause Anne a great deal of trouble.

.... ∾ ....

Anne Hutchinson was born Anne Marbury in July, 1591. She was the second of 13 children. She learned **folk medicine** and healing from her mother, Bridget. She learned to read and to ask questions from her father, Francis. He also taught her to speak up for what she believed. He felt that women had rights like men. Most people did not agree with him.

Anne married William Hutchinson in 1612. She continued to ask questions. Anne became interested in a religious group called the **Puritans**. The Hutchinsons sailed to America with a group of Puritans in 1634. They were seeking religious freedom and felt they needed to leave England to find it.

Anne and her family settled in the **Massachusetts Bay Colony** in New England. Anne was well liked. Women were grateful to her for helping heal them when they were sick. She also delivered their babies.

But Anne was troubled. She felt people in the new land still did not have religious freedom, especially women. She started holding meetings for women in her home. She shared her beliefs about God and the Bible. Before long, the size of the group grew. Even several men started to attend.

In 1637, John Winthrop became governor. He was afraid people would listen to Anne instead of to him. He had Anne arrested. She was pregnant, but she had to stand for hours answering questions. She argued well, and it looked like she might go free. But one of the men from the *Griffin* was there. He told the court Anne had claimed God spoke to her on the ship. The court said this was **heresy** and **banished** Anne

TIDBITS

When Anne left Massachusetts, she was almost forty-seven and five months pregnant. The trip was difficult because of a cold and snowy April. She often had to walk through snow that was up to her thighs. When the group reached Portsmouth, they lived in holes dug in the ground to keep warm until houses were built. They put wooden planks on the bottom of the holes and used tree bark to line the muddy walls.

from Massachusetts. She was also **excommunicated** from her church. Anne walked out of the trial with her head held high. She said, "The Lord judgeth not as man judgeth."

Anne, her family, and 50 to 60 followers went to Rhode Island, where she knew she would have religious freedom. They established what is now Portsmouth, Rhode Island. She continued teaching her beliefs there.

Anne's husband, William, died in 1642. He had been her closest friend, greatest supporter, and lifelong partner. She wanted to be safe from the Puritans in Massachusetts, so she left Rhode Island and moved to New Amsterdam. A year later, Anne and five of her children were killed in an Indian attack.

Anne was only 52 when she died, but she accomplished a great deal. She was the co-founder of Rhode Island. She fought bravely for religious freedom. And she was one of the first Americans to fight for equal rights for women.

The trial of Anne Hutchinson.

TIDBITS

Because of the trial and the difficult journey, not long after Anne reached Rhode Island, she became ill and lost her baby. It would have been her 16th child.

Four presidents, Franklin Delano Roosevelt, Theodore Roosevelt, George Herbert Walker Bush, and George Walker Bush were descendants of Anne Hutchinson.

Anne Hutchinson helped to make Rhode Island the seat of religious freedom in the New World.

Timeline: Anne Hutchinson

1591 ➢ July, Anne Marbury is born in the tiny market town of Alford, Lincolnshire, England to Francis and Bridget Dryden Marbury.

1605 ➢ The family moves to London.

1612 ➢ August 9, Anne marries William Hutchinson, a merchant, and returns to Alford.

1634 ➢ Anne sails for the Massachusetts Bay Colony with her husband and 11 children.

1635 ➢ Anne begins holding meetings for women in her home.

1637 ➢ May, John Winthrop is elected governor of the Massachusetts Bay Colony.

November, Anne is brought to trial for causing religious disharmony.

November 8, the court convicts Anne of heresy and banishes her. She is imprisoned in a home two miles away from her family until the weather is more favorable to send a pregnant woman into the wilderness.

1638 ➢ March 15, Anne is released from her home confinement and summoned to the First Church of Boston for a church trial. She still refuses to admit her beliefs are wrong.

March 22, Anne is excommunicated from the First Church of Boston.

March 28, Anne leaves Massachusetts, and establishes a colony on the island of Aquidneck (which is now Portsmouth, RI).

1639 ➢ In Aquidneck, Anne resumes her religious meetings.

1642 ➢ William Hutchinson dies. Anne leaves Aquidneck for a Dutch settlement in New Amsterdam near present-day Pelham Bay, NY.

1643 ➢ Anne Hutchinson and five of her children are killed by Native Americans at war with the Dutch.

1911 ➢ A bronze tablet is placed at the spot where Anne was killed.

1945 ➢ The Massachusetts legislature votes to revoke Anne's banishment.

1987 ➢ Michael Dukakis, governor of Massachusetts, formally pardons Anne.

1996 ➢ April, a plaque is placed at Founders Brook Park on Aquidneck Island acknowledging Anne's role in founding Portsmouth, RI.

Learn More About Anne Hutchinson and the Puritans

- Clark, Beth. ***Anne Hutchinson: Religious Leader.*** Chelsea House, 2000.
- Mangal, Mélina. ***Anne Hutchinson: Religious Reformer.*** Capstone, 2004.
- Stille, Darlene R. ***Anne Hutchinson: Puritan Protester.*** Compass Point, 2006.

Web sites:

- Pictures and information about the life of and memorials to Anne Hutchinson: http://homepages.rootsweb.ancestry.com/~sam/marbury/anne.html
- Information about the Puritans: http://www.nd.edu/~rbarger/www7/puritans.html
- A page from state of Rhode Island web site regarding Anne Hutchinson's life: http://sos.ri.gov/library/history/famous/hutchinson/

Glossary

banished (BAN isht) Sent away from a place and ordered not to return.

excommunicated (eks kuh MYOO nuh kate id) Cut off officially from a church.

folk medicine (FOHK MED uh suhn) Using plants or animal parts to heal an illness. This type of healing was taught from one person to another before the use of scientific methods.

heresy (HER uh see) Having an opinion or belief that is opposite of a certain church or religion.

Massachusetts Bay Colony One of the first British colonies established in Massachusetts. Today, Boston and Salem, Massachusetts are located in the area once settled by Puritan colonists.

Puritans (PYOOR uh tuhnz) One of a group of English Protestants in the 16th and 17th centuries who believed in a strict code of behavior and who believed worship should be simple, without music and ceremony.

revelation (REV uh LAY shuhn) Surprising information that is made known to someone.

— 2 —

Ann Smith Franklin: Colonial Printer

by Linda Crotta Brennan

Ann Franklin's husband, James, was dead. She led town officials down to her husband's printing press. It was in the basement of the Newport school house. She knew her eldest son, James Junior, was trying to be strong. But he was only ten.

The officials made a list of her husband's belongings. There wasn't much. A stack of unsold books. Some printed songs, a few pamphlets. Four **reams** of paper, **lampblack** for ink, assorted **type**, and leather skins for book covers. How would Ann ever support herself and four small children?

Back in 1718, James Senior had opened a printing press in Boston. He published a newspaper, the *New England Courant*. What he wrote in it often got him into trouble. The year before Ann married James, he was jailed because he complained about the leaders of Massachusetts Bay Colony.

A week after Ann and James married, he was in trouble again. This time it was for making fun of religion. The officials said James had to let them check the paper before he published it. He refused. So they told him he couldn't print the newspaper any more.

James published the paper anyhow under his younger brother Ben's name. Ben worked as his **apprentice.** But Ben didn't like how James treated him. Ben ran away and started his own printing press in Philadelphia. (Ben Franklin later became famous. He grew up to sign the Declaration of Independence.)

James learned that Rhode Island needed a printer. So Ann and James moved to Newport, Rhode Island.

Ann and James had five children, but one died as an infant. Ann cared for their other children and worked alongside her husband. She **set type**. She sold the papers and books. She and James also created a new product. It was printed fabric.

After James died, Ann had to run the printing press alone. She wrote to the Rhode Island government, saying she was a widow with small children. Rhode Island made her the official printer for the colony. Ann printed legal papers, ballots, and Rhode Island laws. She even printed money.

Ann sent James Jr. to Philadelphia to learn from his Uncle Ben. Meanwhile her young daughters helped her at the print shop. Ann also bought a slave to help with the work.

Almanacs were popular then. These booklets included a calendar, moon phases, weather predictions, and **quotations**.

TIDBITS

Following an old tradition, Ann wrote her almanac under a fake name, "Poor Robin." In between the calendars and charts, she wove humorous stories about "Old Moll" and her husband "Tom."

Historians think that Ann may have also carved woodcuts to make illustrations for her printing press.

Ann and James were some of the first fabric printers in America. They printed images, probably with cloth dye, on linen, calico, and silk.

Ann was the first woman in North America to write and publish an almanac.

James Jr. returned from his apprenticeship with his Uncle Ben. He helped his mother with the print shop. They started a newspaper, the *Newport Mercury*. Ann was only the second woman in the Americas to publish a newspaper.

As she got older, Ann let James Jr. run the print shop. But when she was 65, James Jr. died. By then, all her other children were dead, too. Ann took over the print shop again. Though she wasn't well, she didn't skip a single issue of her newspaper. She died the next year at 66.

Her **obituary** said she was a kind and honest woman who supported herself and her family. The *Newport Mercury* is still published today, making it one of the oldest newspapers in the United States.

The Newport Historical Society in Rhode Island displays this Franklin Press.

THE
CHARTER
Granted by His MAJESTY
King CHARLES II.
TO
The Governor and Company
OF
The English COLONY
OF
Rhode-Island
AND
PROVIDENCE-Plantations,
IN NEW-ENGLAND
IN
AMERICA.

A Sample of printing done by Ann Franklin.

TIDBITS

Ann also published books. Many were titles that were popular in Great Britain such as *The Chronicle of the Kings of England* written by Nathan Ben Saddi. The books were marked "reprinted by the Widow Franklin."

Two hundred years after her death, Ann Smith Franklin was the first woman to be elected into the Journalism Hall of Fame at the University of Rhode Island.

Timeline: Ann Smith Franklin

1696 ➤ October 2, Ann Smith is born in Boston. Her parents are Samuel and Anna Smith.

1697 ➤ James Franklin, eldest brother of Benjamin Franklin, is born.

1718 ➤ Ann's brother-in-law, Benjamin Franklin, becomes an apprentice at James' printing press.

1721 ➤ James Franklin publishes the *New England Courant* newspaper in Boston.

1722 ➤ James is jailed for three weeks.

1723 ➤ February 4, Ann marries James Franklin.

February, Massachusetts orders James to stop publishing the *New England Courant.* He continues publishing the paper in his brother Benjamin's name.

September 25, Benjamin runs away to Philadelphia.

1726 ➤ Ann and her husband James leave Boston and move to Newport, RI, staying in the home of James' brother John, who makes candles.

1727 ➤ James and Ann set up the first printing press in RI in two basement rooms of the Newport school house.

1728–1735 ➤ The Franklins print an almanac, written by Joseph Stafford, published under the name "Poor Robin."

1732 ➤ September 27-May 24, 1733, James publishes the *Rhode Island Gazette*, RI's first newspaper.

1735 ➤ February 4, Ann's husband, James, dies. Ann takes over the print shop as "the Widow Franklin."

1737–1741 ➤ Ann **revives** the *Rhode Island Almanack*, writing, editing, and printing it.

1744 ➤ Ann prints Rhode Island's ballots and many other legal documents.

1745 ➤ Ann prints 500 copies of the Acts and Laws of Rhode Island.

1748 ➤ Her son James Franklin Jr. becomes Ann's partner in the print shop.

1758 ➤ June, Ann and James Jr. publish the first issue of the *Newport Mercury*, one of the most important newspapers in the American colonies.

1762 ➤ April, her son, James Franklin Jr., dies.

1763 ➤ April 16, Ann Smith Franklin dies in Newport, Rhode Island.

Learn More About Ann Smith Franklin and Printing In Colonial Times

- Westerman, Karen T. ***John Peter Zenger: Free Press Advocate***. Chelsea House Publishers, 2001.
- Wilmore, Kathy, ***A Day in the Life of a Colonial Printer***. Power Kids Press, 2000.

Web sites:

- "James & Ann Smith Franklin:" http://docsouth.unc.edu/neh/eldridge/summary.html
- "Ann Smith Franklin," *Unseen Hands*: http://infoshare1.princeton.edu/rbsc2/ga/unseenhands/printers/Franklin.html
- Ann Franklin: Colonial Newspaper Printer and Publisher: http://www.womenhistoryblog.com/2008/11/ann-smith-franklin.html

Glossary

almanac (AWL muh nak) A book that is published once a year and contains facts about weather, growing seasons, along with stories and wise sayings.

apprentice (uh PREN tiss) Someone who learns a trade or craft by working with a skilled person.

lampblack (LAMP blak) Black soot or ash that has been ground into a powder to make paints or inks.

obituary (oh BI chuh wair ee) A printed notice about a person's death that usually includes a short biography of the person's life.

quotations (kwoh TAY shuhnz) Sentences taken from a book, play, or a person's speech.

reams (REEMZ) Stacks of papers containing about 500 sheets per stack.

revives (re VIVEZ) In this story, to bring back to use.

set type (SET TIPE) Putting a book or other piece of writing into typed form so it can be used in printing.

type (TIPE) In this story, small metal blocks with raised letters, numbers, and punctuation marks that are coated in ink and used to print newspapers, books, etc.

— 3 —

Elleanor Eldridge: Laborer and Businesswoman

by Sally Wilkins

On a summer evening in 1739, five young white women gathered in the garden of a middle-aged black woman who had worked for all their families.

"I do miss the plants Mr. Balch took," Ellen said.

"It's shameful the way he treated you," Agnes fumed.

"We're here to make another book," Nora said.

Ellen led the friends up the stairs to her apartment. Frances Whipple, the writer, sat in the best chair. The others crowded on to the sofa, with Ellen in the middle. "I've sold 1900 copies of the first book," Ellen said, "If this one sells as well, I believe I will be safe."

Elleanor Eldridge was born in Warwick, Rhode Island in 1785. Her father, Robin, was an African slave. He won his freedom by fighting in the war against the British. Her mother, Hannah, was part Narragansett Indian. Hannah worked as a **laundress**, taking her babies with her to work. Elleanor was named for Elleanor Baker, one of Hannah's employers. Everyone called her Ellen.

Hannah died when Ellen was ten. The Baker family asked Ellen to be their live-in servant. Ellen agreed to work for the Bakers for 25 cents a week. She helped with the cows and chickens. She managed all the laundry. She learned to **spin** and weave.

At 16, Ellen went to work for another Warwick family, the Greenes. After a year of spinning, she began managing their dairy. She made wonderful cheeses.

Captain Greene died in 1806. Ellen and her sister started a business of weaving, soap-making and laundering. Three years later, Ellen moved to Providence. She worked at **whitewashing**, painting and wallpapering in summer, and laundering in winter. Ellen saved her money and bought some land. She built a house big enough for herself and a tenant.

During the next ten years, Ellen borrowed money to build or buy several more houses. She used the rent from her tenants to pay her **creditors**.

Once, while visiting family in Massachusetts, Ellen became very ill. When she came home, she learned a creditor, John Carder, had claimed her property. Carder said he thought Ellen was dead.

Next Ellen went to Connecticut for two months as a nurse. John Carder convinced William Mann, the sheriff, to **auction** off her property. Ellen returned to find her house had been sold to Benjamin Balch. Her tenants had been thrown out.

TIDBITS

When Ellen took the job at the Baker's for 25 cents per week, the average wage for a working man was about $2 per week.

As a teenager Elleanor fell in love with a cousin, called Christopher in the *Memoirs*. He traveled to the West Indies in search of work. He sent letters between his visits home. Christopher was lost at sea in about 1812. Elleanor never married.

Ellen sued both Mann and Balch. The day before his trial, Balch offered to sell the house to her. Ellen borrowed money from many people. Three times, Balch raised the price. In the end, Ellen paid $2700 to buy back her house.

Frances Whipple wrote down Elleanor's story. Many women wrote letters saying Ellen was honest and hard-working. The letters and story became the *Memoirs of Elleanor Eldridge*. A year later, Frances Whipple and her young friends put together *Elleanor's Second Book*.

Ellen sold enough books to pay back all her loans. She continued to work hard and save her earnings. She even bought more houses to rent. When Ellen died in 1862, she was one of the wealthiest black people in Providence.

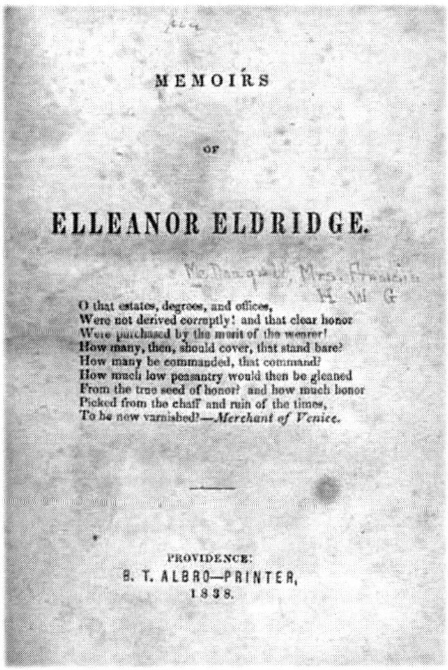
MEMOIRS

OF

ELLEANOR ELDRIDGE.

O that estates, degrees, and offices,
Were not derived corruptly! and that clear honor
Were purchased by the merit of the wearer!
How many, then, should cover, that stand bare?
How many be commanded, that command?
How much low peasantry would then be gleaned
From the true seed of honor? and how much honor
Picked from the chaff and ruin of the times,
To be new varnished?—*Merchant of Venice.*

PROVIDENCE:
B. T. ALBRO—PRINTER,
1838.

The title page of the Memoirs of Elleanor Eldridge *published in 1838.*

TIDBITS

Elleanor traveled up and down the East coast, selling her books in Boston, New York, Philadelphia and many towns and cities in between. She probably traveled and stayed with **Quaker** families.

The *Memoirs* were written to appeal to people who fought against slavery. *Elleanor's Second Book* was slightly different and intended for readers interested in women's rights.

Timeline: Elleanor Eldridge

1785 ➤	March 26, Elleanor Eldridge is born in Warwick, youngest daughter of Robin and Hannah (Prophet) Eldridge (It is sometimes spelled Eldrich).
1795 ➤	Elleanor's mother dies. Elleanor lives and works at the Joseph Baker farm.
1792 ➤	Elleanor begins working for the family of Capt. Benjamin Greene.
1804 ➤	Elleanor's father dies. She travels to Adams, Massachusetts to obtain paperwork from her aunt and surviving siblings and settles his estate.
1806 ➤	Capt. Greene dies. Elleanor moves back to Warwick and goes into business with her sister.
1809 ➤	Elleanor moves to Providence and works painting and wallpapering.
1826 ➤	Elleanor buys land and builds a house with two apartments.
1831 ➤	October, while visiting her family in Massachusetts, Elleanor becomes seriously ill. A rumor starts in Providence that she may have died.
1832 ➤	April, Elleanor returns to Providence from Massachusetts.
	August, Elleanor posts bond for her brother and (over the next 2 years) successfully represents him in court against charges of having attacked a traveler on the highway.
1835 ➤	January, John Carder tries to have Elleanor arrested for failure to pay her debt.
	August, during a **cholera** epidemic in Providence, Elleanor travels to Pomfret, CT as a nurse for a sick child. The sheriff auctions off her property without notifying her or her family.
1837 ➤	Elleanor represents herself in a lawsuit against William Mann, the sheriff who auctioned her property.
1838 ➤	Elleanor dictates her story to Frances Whipple. The *Memoirs of Elleanor Eldridge* is very popular. Four **editions** of the book are sold.
1839 ➤	Elleanor sues Benjamin Balch for **trespass** and the unlawful **ejection** of her tenants from her house.
1842 ➤	*Elleanor's Second Book* sells well enough to merit a second edition in 1845.
1862 ➤	Elleanor dies in Providence at age 76. Her nieces and nephews inherit $4500.

Learn More About Elleanor Eldridge and Life as a Free Black American before the Civil War

- Brennan, Linda Crotta. ***The Black Regiment of The American Revolution.*** Apprentice Shop Books, 2008.
- Hakim, Joy. ***The New Nation***. Oxford UP, 2005.
- Kamma, Anne and Pamela Johnson. ***If You Lived When There Was Slavery in America***. Scholastic, 2006.

Web sites:

- A summary of the life of Elleanor Eldridge: http://docsouth.unc.edu/neh/eldridge/summary.html
- Read Elleanor's book: http://archive.org/details/memoirsofelleanore00eldr

Glossary

auction (AWK shuhn) A sale where goods are sold to the person who offers the most money for them.

cholera (KOL ur uh) A dangerous disease that causes severe sickness and diarrhea.

creditors (KRED it urz) People who loan money to others.

editions (i DISH uhnz) Different versions of a book.

ejection (i JEKT shuhn) The act of being thrown out of something.

laundress (LAWN druhss) A woman who washes and irons clothes for others.

Quaker (KWAY kur) A member of the Society of Friends, a Christian group founded in 1650 that prefers simple religious services and opposes war.

spin (SPIN) To use a machine to turn fibers into yarn or thread.

trespass (TRESS pass) To go into private property without the owner's permission.

whitewashing (WITE wosh ing) Using a mixture of lime and water to create a kind of white paint for walls, wooden shingles, or wooden fences.

— 4 —

Prudence Crandall: Fighter for Equal Rights to Education

by Linda Crotta Brennan

A friend of Prudence Crandall's **housekeeper** came to the door. Her name was Sarah Harris. She pleaded, "Miss Crandall, I want to get a little more learning..."

What could Prudence say? Her school for young ladies only taught white girls. Sarah Harris was black.

Miss Crandall didn't answer right away. She had worked hard. Her school had an excellent **reputation**. Could she risk it all by taking in a black student?

Prudence Crandall was born in 1803 in Hopkinton, Rhode Island. Later, her father bought a farm in Canterbury, Connecticut. He moved the family there. Her parents were **Quakers**. They believed in educating both their sons and daughters. They sent Prudence to a Quaker school in Providence, Rhode Island.

Prudence became a teacher. She rejoined her family in Connecticut. She opened Canterbury Female **Boarding School** to teach young ladies.

Many wealthy people sent their daughters there.

If Prudence let Sarah Harris attend classes, her students' parents would be angry. But how could Prudence say no? Her Quaker religion taught that all people were equal.

Prudence agreed to let Sarah come to class. The parents of Miss Crandall's white students protested. They threatened to take their daughters out. Send Sarah away, they said, or the school will sink.

So Prudence closed her school for white girls. She opened a school for "young ladies and little misses of color" instead. Black girls from all over New England came to her school. Girls from New York and Pennsylvania came too.

The people of Canterbury didn't want a school for African-Americans in their town. They shouted and threw things at Prudence's students. Shopkeepers refused to sell the school food or supplies. They held town meetings to try to close her school down.

One of Prudence Crandall's neighbors was Andrew Judson. He was an important lawyer. He convinced the Connecticut **legislature** to pass the "Black Law." The law said it was illegal to teach black students from out of state.

Many of Ms. Crandall's students came from out of state. Her school broke the "Black Law." She was arrested and went to trial. Meanwhile, the townspeople threw rocks through the school windows. They dumped manure down Prudence's well. Someone even tried to set the school on fire.

Prudence's lawyer argued that the "Black Law" was against

TIDBITS

When Prudence Crandall opened her school for African-American girls, slavery was legal in the south. Slavery was illegal in most northern states, but that didn't mean northerners thought African-Americans were equal to whites.

Prudence's first black student, Sarah Harris, eventually married and moved to Kingston, Rhode Island. She and her husband were **abolitionists**. They were conductors on the **Underground Railroad**.

the Constitution. It granted citizens the freedom to travel from one state to another. Andrew Judson argued that African Americans weren't citizens. Prudence's case went through multiple **appeals**.

A minister named Calvin Philleo attended many of these trials. He started to **woo** Prudence. Her friends didn't trust him. But Prudence agreed to marry him.

Finally, Prudence Crandall was found not guilty. She won her case. But the court refused to say that African Americans were citizens.

Now Prudence was free to run her school. She and Reverend Philleo wed. But a few months later, more trouble came. Shouts woke Prudence, her husband, and her students. A mob smashed the windows. Wild men stormed through classrooms.

Prudence decided she couldn't keep her school open. It was too dangerous for her girls. She and her husband sold the school and left Connecticut.

Prudence and her husband moved often. Reverend Philleo was sickly. He was also mentally ill. After he died, Prudence went with her brother to Elk Falls, Kansas. She continued to teach and fight for human rights until her death at 87.

The statue of Prudence Crandall and an African American student is located in the Connecticut State Capitol.

TIDBITS

When she was 83 years old, Prudence received a telegram from the state of Connecticut. It apologized for what happened to her and her school. The state granted her a pension for life.

In recent years, Connecticut school children started a petition. They asked that Prudence Crandall be named the official state heroine. This request was granted on October 1, 1995.

Timeline: Prudence Crandall

1803 ➤ September 3, Prudence Crandall is born to Esther and Pardon Crandall in Hopkington, RI. She is the second of four children.

1831 ➤ Prudence Crandall opens the Canterbury Female Boarding School.

1832 ➤ September, African-American Sarah Harris asks to attend Miss Crandall's school.

1833 ➤ January, Sarah becomes a student at Prudence Crandall's school.

March, Miss Crandall closes the Canterbury Female Boarding School.

April, she reopens it as a school for "young ladies and little misses of color."

May 24, the state of Connecticut enacts the "Black Law."

1834 ➤ January, Prudence's school is set on fire.

July, the case against Prudence Crandall is dismissed.

August 12, Prudence marries Calvin Philleo.

September 9, a mob attacks Prudence Crandall's school.

September 10, Prudence closes the school.

1835 ➤ Prudence and her husband leave Connecticut and go to Ithaca, NY.

1838 ➤ The "Black Law" is repealed.

1874 ➤ Prudence's husband Calvin Philleo dies.

1877 ➤ Prudence and her brother Hezekiah move to Elks Falls, Kansas.

1886 ➤ Connecticut apologizes to Prudence Crandall and grants her a pension for life.

1890 ➤ January 28, Prudence Crandall dies at age 87 in Elk Falls, Kansas.

1995 ➤ October 1, Prudence Crandall is declared the official state heroine of Connecticut.

Learn More About Prudence Crandall

- Alexander, Elizabeth and Marilyn Nelson. ***Miss Crandall's School For Young Ladies & Little Misses of Color: Poems.*** Wordsong, 2007.
- Jurmain, Suzanne. ***Forbidden Schoolhouse: The True and Dramatic Story of Prudence and Her Students.*** Houghton Mifflin Co., 2005.
- Lucas, Eileen. ***Prudence Crandall: Teacher for Equality.*** Carolrhoda Books, 2001.

Web sites:

- The Prudence Crandall Museum: http://www.cultureandtourism.org/cct/cwp/view.asp?a=2127&q=302260

Glossary

abolitionist (AB uh LISH uh nist) Abolitionists opposed slavery and worked to have it abolished (ended) in the United States.

appeals (uh PEELZ) Requests to take a case to a higher court for review.

boarding school (BORD ing SKOOL) A school that students may live in during the school year.

housekeeper (HOUS kee per) A woman in charge of running a home and keeping it clean.

legislature (LEJ iss LAY chur) A group of elected people who have the power to make or change laws for a state or country.

Quaker (KWAY kur) A member of the Society of Friends, a Christian group founded in 1650 that prefers simple religious services and opposes war.

reputation (REP yuh TAY shuhn) A person's character as it is seen by other people.

Underground Railroad (UHN dur ground RAYL rohd) A group of people who secretly helped Southern slaves escape to free Northern states or Canada. The Underground Railroad existed before the American Civil War.

woo (WOO) To court or try to attract in hopes that the other person will fall in love.

— 5 —

Frances Harriet Whipple Green McDougall: Writer for Those in Need

by Linda Crotta Brennan

A group of Frances' society friends came to call. A woman who worked for them was in trouble. She was an African-American and **Narragansett** woman named Elleanor Eldridge. A white man was trying to cheat her of her property. Elleanor was hardworking, "honest and faithful." Could Frances help her?

Frances Harriet Whipple was born in Smithfield, Rhode Island in 1805. Her parents came from wealthy Rhode Island families. When Frances was twelve, her father lost all his property. Her parents moved to a farm. They struggled to earn a living. They left Frances in Smithfield to take care of herself.

Historians don't know what Frances did. She probably lived with relatives. She might have worked as a servant. She may have worked in a mill.

When she was 24, Frances started a magazine, *The Original.* It included poetry, histories, essays, and stories. Frances wrote most of the

TIDBITS

Frances' books about Elleanor Eldridge are some of the few sources we have about what life was like for a free black woman before the Civil War.

•◆•

In her second book about Elleanor Eldridge, Frances wrote that she hoped the reader would not allow "... *an unoffending citizen [to be] robbed of her rights even though she be a woman—and a colored woman.*"

pieces. One essay was about the importance of education. Another story told about poor Irish people who came to America. *The Original* lasted for only two issues. But Frances kept writing.

Friends came to Frances with the tale of Elleanor Eldridge's problems. Frances told them that she would write Elleanor's biography. Frances hoped it would "render some little assistance. . . ."

Frances wrote a book about Elleanor's life. It earned money, but not quite enough. Frances wrote a second book about Elleanor. Frances gave the money from her book sales to Elleanor. Elleanor was able to get back her property.

Frances championed many causes. A friend said Frances "listened with tearful emotion to every tale of suffering." She wrote books against slavery. She edited a magazine for factory workers. Frances wrote to support **temperance**. Temperance groups were against drinking alcohol.

In 1842, Thomas Dorr led a **rebellion** in Rhode Island. He was trying to gain broader voting rights. Thomas Dorr was put in prison. Frances wrote a book to aid him. The book turned some people against her.

Frances also wrote poetry. Her most famous poem was "Roger Williams." He was the founder of Rhode Island. Schoolchildren recited this poem to celebrate Rhode Island Independence Day.

When she was 36, Frances married a 24-year-old artist. His name was Charles Green. Five years later, she divorced him. She accused him of cruelty. She said he abandoned her.

A few months after her divorce, Frances moved to New York. She lived with the family of Reverend Samuel Brittan. He was a **spiritualist.** Spiritualists believed that the dead could communicate with the living. Frances became an **editor** of Brittan's spiritualist journal. She wrote the biography of a **medium** named Semantha Mettler.

Frances was also interested in plants. She taught plant study for many years. She wrote two textbooks on the subject for her students.

When she was 55, Frances moved to California. There she met and married a miner, William C. McDougall.

She wrote her last book with another woman. It was called *Beyond the Veil.* The book was about the after-life of Pascal Beverly Randolf. He was an African-American spiritualist. Frances claimed that his spirit spoke to her after his death. He directed her to write the book.

Frances died at the home of friends in 1878 at the age of 73. *Beyond the Veil* was published after her death.

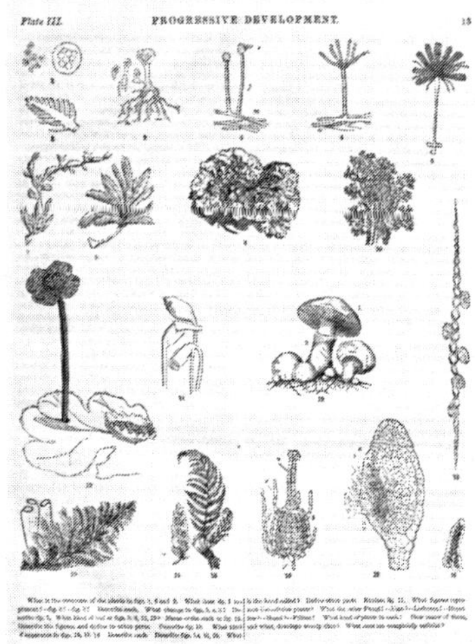

A page from Harriet's book on plant studies.

TIDBITS

In 1841, only white males who owned property could vote in Rhode Island. That was less than half of the men. Thomas Dorr wanted to extend **suffrage** to landless white males. The privileged males who could vote fought him.

Spiritualism was popular in America from 1850-1870. Spiritualists believed that mediums could go into a **trance** and communicate with the dead.

Timeline: Frances Harriet Whipple Green McDougall

1805 ➤ September, Frances is born in Smithfield, RI to George and Ann Whipple.

1829 ➤ May, and 1830, January, Frances publishes a magazine called *The Original.*

1838 ➤ She writes *Memoirs of Elleanor Eldridge,* the biography of a free black woman.

1840 ➤ Frances writes *The Envoy: From Free Hearts to the Free,* an anti-slavery book for children.

1842 ➤ July 1, Frances marries artist Charles C. Green.

She publishes *The Mechanic,* a book about the working classes. She begins as editor of the *Wampanoag and Operatives Journal,* a magazine for Fall River mill workers. She writes *Elleanor's Second Book.*

1844 ➤ Frances writes *Might and Right,* a defense of Thomas Dorr who is in prison for his 1842 rebellion for broader voting rights in Rhode Island.

1845 ➤ She contributes to *Liberty Chimes*, a publication of the Ladies Anti-Slavery Society of Providence, RI.

1847 ➤ September, Frances divorces Charles Green.

1848–1849 ➤ She co-manages the *Young People's Journal* of science, literature, and art.

1852–1854 ➤ Frances contributes to the spiritualist journal, *Shekinah.*

1853 ➤ She writes the *Biography of Mrs. Semantha Mettler, the Clairvoyant.*

1856 ➤ Frances publishes a book on the study of plants.

1858 ➤ She publishes *Shahmah in Pursuit of Freedom* or *The Branded Hand*, a book against slavery.

1860 ➤ Frances moves to California.

1861 ➤ She marries William C. McDougall.

1878 ➤ June 10, Frances Whipple Green McDougall dies at age 73.

Her last book, *Beyond the Veil: Posthumous Work of Pascal Beverly Randolf* is published after her death.

Learn More About Frances Harriet Whipple Green McDougall and Her Causes:

- Edwards, Judith. ***Abolitionists And Slave Resistance: Breaking The Chains Of Slavery***, Enslow, 2004.
- Isaacs, Sally Senzell. ***Life In A New England Mill Town***, Heinemen Library, 2003.
- Slavicek, Louise Chipley. ***The Prohibition Era: Temperance In The United States***, Chelsea House, 2009.

Web sites:

- A short biography of Frances Harriet Whipple Green McDougall: http://faculty.ccri.edu/rprisco/RIWA/riwomenspeak/bookscans/frances_harriet_whipple_green_mcdougall.html
- A story about the Dorr Rebellion: http://www.woonsocket.org/dorrwar.html

Glossary

editor (ED uh tur) Someone who checks the contents of a book, newspaper, or magazine and gets it ready to be published.

historians (hi STOR ee uhnz) Students or writers of history.

medium (MEE dee uhm) In this story, someone who claims to be able to communicate with the dead.

Narragansett (NER uh GAN sit) The native people of the State of Rhode Island. These warriors came to the Rhode Island area over 3,000 years ago.

rebellion (ri BEL yuhn) An armed fight against people who are in charge.

Spiritualist (SPIHR uh CHOO uh list) Spiritualists believed the living could be helped by the spirits of the dead.

suffrage (SUHF rij) The right to vote.

temperance (TEM pruhnss) A movement that urged people not to drink alcoholic beverages.

trance (TRANSS) A sleep-like state in which a person is conscious but not aware of his or her surroundings.

— 6 —

Elizabeth Buffum Chace:

Activist and Reformer

by Barbara J. Turner

Elizabeth stood in the darkened room with the two young black men. They looked strange in their Quaker clothes, but the disguise had worked before. It would work again. She handed each man an envelope with her name and address on it then her husband led them out the door.

Elizabeth waited and waited. One day passed. Then two. On the fourth day, the envelopes arrived. The **postmark** was from Canada. They were free!

.... ᘏ ....

Elizabeth Buffam was born in Providence, Rhode Island on December 9, 1806. Soon after, her family moved to Smithfield, Rhode Island. Her mother cared for the family. Her father made and sold hats.

The Buffams were **Quakers** and **abolitionists.** They believed all people were equal and no one should be a slave. Elizabeth grew up listening to anti-slavery speeches. She learned acceptance.

When she was six, her father's business failed. Elizabeth was put to work in a **textile mill** to help support her family. She worked until her father found another job. She learned responsibility. She also had an uncle who was mentally ill. Her grandmother kept him in an upstairs room. When Elizabeth visited her, she often stood in the yard and watched him staring out his window at her. She learned compassion

Elizabeth grew up and married Samuel Buffington Chace. He was a Quaker and abolitionist, too. They moved to Massachusetts where Samuel owned a mill. Elizabeth formed the Ladies' Anti-slavery Society of Fall River while she was there. She hoped to help free the slaves.

But even abolitionists weren't quite ready to do that. Many of them thought slaves should be educated first. Or they should have homes or jobs. One man, William Garrison, didn't agree. He believed all slaves should be freed immediately. He wrote about it in his newspaper, the *Liberator*. Elizabeth believed he was right.

In 1837, Samuel's business failed. The Chaces moved back to Rhode Island. Elizabeth continued her work there. She spoke out against slavery. She made her home a stop on the **Underground Railroad.** She helped runaway slaves reach Canada and freedom.

Many of Elizabeth's Quaker friends thought she went too far. They began to avoid her. Some crossed the street if they saw her coming. This saddened Elizabeth. Still, she had to do what she believed was right. She left the Quakers.

Elizabeth worked hard for the freedom of slaves until the Civil War ended and slavery was **abolished.** But she didn't

TIDBITS

By the time she was forty-five, Elizabeth had given birth to ten children. The first five died before they reached their teens. Of the five who survived, two died in their early twenties. Only three of Elizabeth's children outlived her.

Elizabeth's resignation from the Quakers caused a bit of confusion. The Quakers said she had not resigned, because she couldn't. There was no precedent. Elizabeth said she could resign because she had.

give up fighting. She fought for women's rights. She fought for prisoners' rights. She fought for the poor. And she fought for children.

Elizabeth realized many prisoners had children. Those children often ended up in **alms houses** or **reform schools**. This angered Elizabeth. The children had done nothing wrong. Why should they be punished?

She began planning a home and school for them. She imagined cozy cottages instead of brick buildings. She saw a school where children were taught things that interested them. Why teach girls to clean if they could become writers and artists? Why teach boys to mend chairs if they could be **architects**?

Elizabeth fought for her school for over thirty years. Finally, in 1884, the Rhode Island Home and School for Dependent Children was built. Elizabeth's dream became a reality.

Elizabeth spent her lifetime helping others. When she died on December 12, 1899, she was hailed as 'the conscience of Rhode Island,' as the woman who cared.

House of Mrs. Elizabeth Buffum Chace, a station of the Underground Railroad, Valley Falls, Rhode Island.

TIDBITS

Elizabeth thought the new 'bloomer' outfit extremely ugly. The style consisted of loose pants, gathered at the ankle, worn under a short skirt. Still, she tried it on to show her support for the women's movement. She found it freeing and comfortable and wore it around the house when she cleaned. One day, she dared to wear it outside in public. She was so self-conscious about its ugliness, she never wore it again. Not even indoors.

Timeline: Elizabeth Buffum Chace

1806 ➤ December 9, Elizabeth Buffam is born in Providence, RI to Quakers Arnold Buffam and Rebecca Gould.

1822 ➤ Elizabeth attends Friends Boarding School in Providence for one year.

1828 ➤ April 4, Elizabeth marries Quaker Samuel B. Chace and moves to Fall River, MA.

1835 ➤ Elizabeth helps found the Ladies' Anti-slavery Society of Fall River.

1837 ➤ Samuel's business fails and the Chaces move to Valley Falls, RI. Elizabeth begins her work on the Underground Railroad.

1844 ➤ Elizabeth leaves the Quakers because they are against anti-slavery activism.

1850 ➤ Elizabeth attends the Worcester Women's Rights Convention and begins her work in that field.

1852 ➤ Elizabeth gives birth to the last of her ten children. The first five all died in childhood.

1858 ➤ The Chaces move to Central Falls, RI.

1865 ➤ The Civil War ends and the slaves are freed. Elizabeth turns her activism toward women's rights and prison reform.

1868 ➤ December 11, Elizabeth forms the Rhode Island Women's Suffrage Association with Paulina W. Davis.

1870 ➤ Elizabeth becomes President of the Rhode Island Women's Suffrage Association, and remains President until her death.

She convinces the state legislature to allow female inspectors in prisons to serve as a Board of Lady Visitors.

1872 ➤ Elizabeth is a delegate to the World Prison Congress in London, England.

1878 ➤ Elizabeth founds the first kindergarten in Rhode Island, at Valley Falls.

1891 ➤ Elizabeth writes *Anti-slavery Reminiscences.*

1899 ➤ Elizabeth dies and is hailed as 'the conscience of Rhode Island.'

2001 ➤ A bronze bust of Elizabeth is given a place of honor in the Rhode Island State House.

Learn More Elizabeth Buffum Chace and Her Causes

- Landau, Elaine. ***The Abolitionist Movement (Cornerstones of Freedom).*** Children's Press, 2008.
- Kamma, Anne. ***If You Lived When There was Slavery in America.*** Scholastic, 2004.
- Williams, Jean Kinney. ***The Quakers (American Religious Experience).*** Franklin Watts, 1998

Web sites:

- A short history of Elizabeth and her daughter Lillie: http://www.quahog.org/factsfolklore/index.php?id=104
- Information about slavery, abolitionists, and Quakers: http://www.pbs.org/wnet/slavery/timeline/index.html

Glossary

abolished (uh BOL ishd) Put an end to something officially. The 13th Amendment to the U.S. Constitution abolished slavery.

abolitionists (AB uh LISH uh nistss) People who worked to end slavery before the Civil War.

alms houses (AMZ houss iz) Homes owned by a town or county where homeless people could live. Often an alms house was supported by a charity.

architects (AR ki tekss) People who draw the designs for buildings.

postmark (POHST mark) An official stamp that is put on a piece of mail to show that the postage has been used.

Quakers (KWAY kurz) Members of the Society of Friends, a Christian group founded in 1650 that prefers simple religious services and opposes war.

reform schools (RI form SKOOL) A jail used to house young boys accused of committing crimes.

textile mill (TEK stile MIL) A factory that produces cloth made by weaving threads together.

Underground Railroad (UHN dur ground RAYL rohd) A group of people who secretly helped Southern slaves escape to free Northern states or Canada. The Underground Railroad existed before the American Civil War.

7

Christiana Carteaux Bannister:

Black Businesswoman and Community Activist

by Cheryl Kirk Noll

Christiana Bannister stood behind the "President's Table." She smoothed her billowing hoop skirts as she looked around busy Mercantile Hall in Boston. She had worked hard, organizing this five day Soldier's Relief Fair. But raising money for the widows and children of **colored** Civil War soldiers was a cause worth fighting for.

The hall was filled with tables **sponsored** by both colored and white ladies' groups. Many of the women were customers at Christiana's hair **salons.** Many of them were part of the **abolitionist** movement. They believed that slavery was wrong.

Christiana's husband also contributed. Edward Bannister was an artist. He painted a life-sized portrait of the white commander of the 54th Colored Regiment. The painting was about to be **raffled.** Christiana was proud that her husband's gift would raise even more money for the soldiers' families.

Christiana Babcock was born in North Kingstown, Rhode Island in 1819. Her parents were Narragansett Indian and Black. She had eight brothers and sisters.

In the 1840s, Christiana married Desiline Carteaux. She moved to Boston and opened her own hair dressing and wig-making salon. She called her business "Madame Carteaux: Hair Doctress."

Christiana's marriage did not last long, but her business was successful. Soon, "Madame Carteaux" opened more salons. She sold her own line of hair products. She advertised in *The Liberator*, an abolitionist newspaper. The newspaper wrote an article about the most successful African-American business people in Boston. Christiana was included.

In 1853, Christiana met Edward Mitchell Bannister. Edward came to Boston to study painting. But he couldn't find an artist who would accept a black student. Christiana hired him as a barber at one of her salons.

Four years later, Christiana and Edward were married. Christiana's **financial** success allowed Edward to paint full-time.

Christiana worked for the needs of black soldiers during the Civil War. She became President of the Colored Ladies Relief Society. A ceremony was held when the 54th Massachusetts Colored Regiment left to fight for the Union. Christiana was asked to "present the colors." She gave the state flag to the regiment's commander. The men carried the flag when they went into battle.

TIDBITS

Christiana was born free in Rhode Island. But slavery was still legal in many states. Although RI banned slavery after the Revolutionary War, they didn't free people who were already slaves. Christiana was 40 years old by the time the last slave in RI died.

Christiana and her husband were part of Boston's black middle-class. They became active in artistic circles. Christiana performed several leading roles in a black theatre club.

The black soldiers were paid less than white soldiers. Christiana fought to get them equal pay. Many of the men were killed or disabled in battle. Christiana raised money for their families.

After the Civil War ended, Christiana moved back to Rhode Island with her husband. For the next thirty years, Christiana ran several successful salons in downtown Providence. Edward became a well-known painter.

One of his paintings won a first-prize medal at the **Philadelphia Centennial Exposition**. Edward gave Christiana credit for his success. He wrote, "I would have made out very poorly had it not been for her, and my greatest successes have come... through her **criticisms** of my pictures or the advice she would give me in the matter of placing them in public."

Christiana continued to work for her community. Black women often had jobs as housekeepers. When they were too old to work any more, many became homeless.

Christiana raised money to help these women. Some of the wealthy customers from her hair salons donated land and furniture. In 1890, the Home for Aged Colored Women opened in Providence. Later, it was renamed Bannister House in Christiana's honor.

Christiana died in 1903.

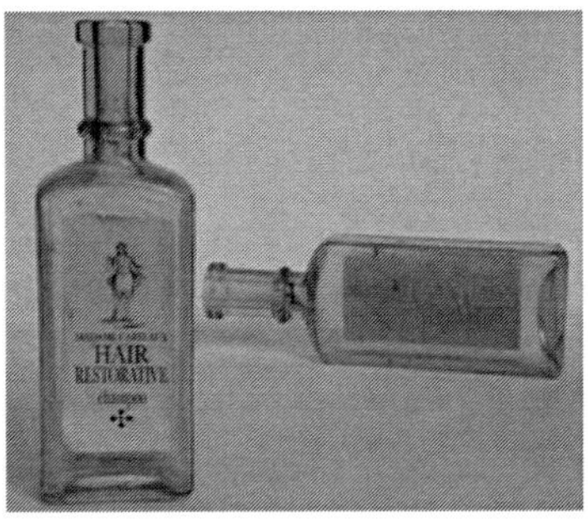

Christiana sold her own brand of "champoo" in bottles like these.

TIDBITS

Christiana and Edward were part of the abolitionist movement in Boston. Christiana's brother-in-law and sister-in-law were well-known speakers at anti-slavery meetings. For two years, Christiana and Edward rented rooms in a house that was part of the **Underground Railroad**.

Timeline: Christiana Carteaux Bannister

1819 ➤ Christiana Babcock is born to Mary and Charles Babcock in North Kingston, Rhode Island.

1840s ➤ Christiana marries Desiline Carteaux, but they are soon divorced.

Christiana opens the first of at least four hairdressing salons in Boston.

1855 ➤ Christiana opens her first salon in Providence, RI.

1857 ➤ June 10, Christiana marries Edward Mitchell Bannister.

1861–1865 ➤ The Bannisters live in Boston during the American Civil War.

1860s ➤ Christiana is President of the Boston's Colored Ladies Relief Society and several related organizations.

1862 ➤ Congress passes acts allowing Blacks to join the armed forces.

1863 ➤ Christiana presents the colors (a state flag) to the commander of the 54th Massachusetts Colored Volunteers Regiment at a ceremony before they leave to fight.

1864 ➤ June 15, Congress passes a bill authorizing equal pay, equipment, arms, and health care for Black Union troops.

October, Christiana organizes the Colored Soldier's Relief Fair.

1869 ➤ The Bannisters move to Providence. Christiana runs a series of hair salons in downtown Providence for the next thirty years.

1890 ➤ Christiana raises enough money to open the Home for Aged Colored Women in Providence.

1901 ➤ Edward Bannister dies.

1903 ➤ Christiana Bannister dies in Cranston, Rhode Island.

2002 ➤ A bust of Christiana Bannister, sculpted by Pablo Eduardo, is unveiled at a ceremony honoring her at the Rhode Island State House.

2010 ➤ March 25, Christiana Carteaux Bannister is honored during Women's History month in Rhode Island.

Learn More About Christiana Bannister's Life and Times

- DeAngelis, Gina. ***The Massachusetts 54th: African American Soldiers of the Union.*** Bridgestone Books, 2003.
- Forten, Charlotte L. ***A Free Black Girl Before the Civil War: The Diary of Charlotte Forten, 1854.*** Blue Earth Books, 2000.
- Lasky, Kathryn. ***Vision of Beauty: The Story of Sarah Breedlove Walker.*** Candlewick Press, 2000.

Web sites:

- Short biographies of black business people including Christiana: http://www.economicadventure.org/exhibits/black-entrepreneurs/black_entrepreneurs_bios.html#CHRISTIANA%20CARTEAUX%20BANNISTER

Glossary

abolitionist (AB uh LISH uh nist) A person who worked to end slavery before the Civil War.

colored A word commonly used during Christiana's lifetime to refer to people of African ancestry and to Native Americans.

criticisms (KRIT uh siz uhmz) Statements that tell the good and bad parts of a work of art, a story, a piece of music, and so on.

financial (fye NAN shuhl) Having to do with money or finances.

Philadelphia Centennial Exposition The first major World's Fair to be held in the United States, opened on May 10, 1876.

raffled (RAF uhld) Sold tickets for prizes that would be given away in order to raise money for a special cause.

salon (suh LAWN) A beauty parlor; a place where one has hair cut or styled.

sponsored (SPON surd) Gave money for a good cause.

Underground Railroad (UHN dur ground RAYL rohd) A group of people who secretly helped Southern slaves escape to free Northern states or Canada. The Underground Railroad existed before the American Civil War.

— 8 —

Julia Ward Howe: Poet and Reformer

by Jo Pitkin

During the Civil War, Julia Ward Howe traveled to Virginia for a review of **Union** troops. On the trip, Julia and her companions sang popular marching songs to pass the time. One friend urged Julia to write words to the tune of "John Brown's Body."

Early the next morning, Julia penned a **patriotic** poem. She recalled, "I awoke in the gray of the morning twilight; and as I lay waiting for the dawn, the long lines of the desired poem began to twine themselves in my mind."

Mine eyes have seen the glory of the coming of the Lord;
He is trampling out the ***vintage*** *where the grapes of wrath are stored;*
He hath loosed the fateful lightning of His terrible swift sword:
His truth is marching on.

Her "Battle Hymn of the Republic" became a **rallying cry** for those—like Julia—who supported the cause against slavery. And it made Julia famous.

Julia Ward was born in New York City in 1819. Her father was a wealthy banker from Rhode Island. Her mother wrote and published poetry. After Julia's mother died, **governesses** and an aunt helped care for Julia and her brothers and sisters.

At home, Julia learned Latin, French, literature, music, and other subjects from private teachers. When she was nine, she went to school. Like most girls at the time, she finished her formal education by sixteen. However, Julia continued her studies on her own.

In 1832, all of the Ward children suffered from a serious illness. They spent that summer in Newport, Rhode Island. Being outdoors near the ocean was good for their health. For the rest of her life, Julia spent nearly every summer in Newport.

Julia married Dr. Samuel Gridley Howe in 1843. Howe was the director of the first school for the blind in the United States. The couple took a **honeymoon** trip to Europe. Nearly two years later, they returned to the United States with the first of their six children. They settled in Boston.

The Howes had a stormy marriage. Samuel did not want Julia to work outside of the home. He did not support her writing. Also, he took charge of Julia's **inheritance** but lost most of it. Julia became more and more unhappy. In 1850, she separated from Samuel. She went to Rome, Italy, with her two younger children. But she eventually **reconciled** with her husband.

In 1853, Julia went against her husband's wishes. She

TIDBITS

Julia began writing as a young girl. When she was 13, she gave her father a book of her poetry. Her first published poems appeared in the magazine *American* when she was 14

In 1879, Julia called for a women's day of protest against war. The first Mother's Peace Day was held on June 2, 1873. Her idea sparked our celebration of Mother's Day. It became a national holiday in 1914.

secretly took her poems to a Boston publisher. Samuel was extremely disturbed when her first book of poetry was published **anonymously** in 1854.

After the Civil War ended in 1865, slavery was outlawed. But Julia became involved in other causes. She believed that women should have the right to vote. She was active in the women's **suffrage** movement. She also fought for world peace, human rights, and prison reform.

Julia's husband died in 1876. Over the next thirty-four years, she had the freedom to pursue a public life. She delivered speeches. She preached sermons. She traveled to Europe and the Middle East. She published essays, a biography, poems, and other writings.

Julia died in 1910 at the age of 91. Four thousand people attended her funeral at Boston's Symphony Hall. Those who mourned Julia honored her by singing her most well-known piece of writing—*"Battle Hymn of the Republic."*

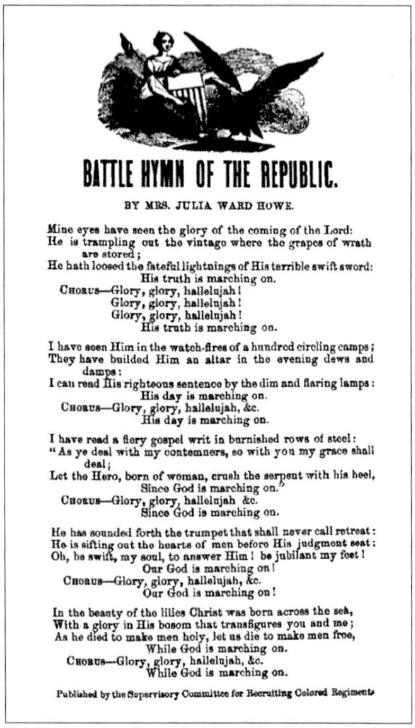

BATTLE HYMN OF THE REPUBLIC.

BY MRS. JULIA WARD HOWE.

Mine eyes have seen the glory of the coming of the Lord:
He is trampling out the vintage where the grapes of wrath are stored;
He hath loosed the fateful lightnings of His terrible swift sword:
His truth is marching on.
CHORUS—Glory, glory, hallelujah!
Glory, glory, hallelujah!
Glory, glory, hallelujah!
His truth is marching on.

I have seen Him in the watch-fires of a hundred circling camps;
They have builded Him an altar in the evening dews and damps:
I can read His righteous sentence by the dim and flaring lamps:
His day is marching on.
CHORUS—Glory, glory, hallelujah, &c.
His day is marching on.

I have read a fiery gospel writ in burnished rows of steel:
"As ye deal with my contemners, so with you my grace shall deal;
Let the Hero, born of woman, crush the serpent with his heel,
Since God is marching on."
CHORUS—Glory, glory, hallelujah &c.
Since God is marching on.

He has sounded forth the trumpet that shall never call retreat:
He is sifting out the hearts of men before His judgment seat:
Oh, be swift, my soul, to answer Him! be jubilant my feet!
Our God is marching on!
CHORUS—Glory, glory, hallelujah, &c.
Our God is marching on!

In the beauty of the lilies Christ was born across the sea,
With a glory in His bosom that transfigures you and me;
As he died to make men holy, let us die to make men free,
While God is marching on.
CHORUS—Glory, glory, hallelujah, &c.
While God is marching on.

Published by the Supervisory Committee for Recruiting Colored Regiments

The lyrics to Julia Ward Howe's Battle Hymn of the Republic.

TIDBITS

Julia's daughters Laura, Maud, and Florence wrote her biography. *Julia Ward Howe, 1819–1910* won the Pulitzer Prize in 1917.

Julia was inducted into the Rhode Island Heritage Hall of Fame in 2003.

Composer Henry Papale created an opera about Julia Ward Howe called *Julia!* The opera, which was based on Julia's letters, was first performed in 2007 in New York's Symphony Space/Thalia Theatre.

Timeline: Julia Ward Howe

1819	May 27, Julia is born in New York City. She is the fourth of Samuel and Julia Rush Cutler Ward's seven children.
1824	Julia's mother dies.
1839	Julia's father dies.
1840	Julia's brother Henry dies.
1843	April 23, Julia marries Dr. Samuel Gridley Howe, the director of the Perkins Institute for the Blind.
1844	Julia's first child, Julia, is born in Rome, Italy.
1845	Her daughter Florence is born.
1848	Julia has a son, Henry.
1850	She has a daughter, Laura.
1854	Julia's book *Passion-Flowers* is published anonymously. Her daughter Maud is born.
1857	Her second book of poetry, *Words for the Hour*, is published. Her play *The World's Own* is performed.
1859	Julia's son Samuel is born.
1860	She publishes *A Trip to Cuba* about her travel experiences.
1861	November, Julia writes "Battle Hymn of the Republic."
1862	February, "Battle Hymn of the Republic" is published in *The Atlantic Monthly*.
1863	Her son Samuel dies.
1866	Julia's third book of poems, *Later Lyrics,* is published.
1876	Julia's husband dies.
1899	She publishes a book about her own life, *Reminiscences 1819–1899*.
1908	Julia is the first woman elected to the American Academy of Arts and Letters.
1910	October 17, Julia Ward Howe dies of pneumonia near Newport, Rhode Island, at the age of 91.

Learn More About Julia Ward Howe and Her Causes

- Raum, Elizabeth. ***Julia Ward Howe***. Heinemann Library, 2004.
- Mosley, Shelley and John Charles. ***The Suffragists in Literature for Youth: The Fight for the Vote.*** The Scarecrow Press, 2006.
- Rappaport, Doreen and Joan Verniero. ***United No More! Stories of the Civil War.*** HarperCollins, 2006.

Web sites:

- A biography of Julia Ward Howe: http://www.juliawardhowe.org/
- Mother's Day For Peace (How Mother's Day began): http://www.youtube.com/watch?v=LtzAwo1HU2w
- Massachusetts Center for the Book Literary Map: http://www.massbook.org/OnlineMap--New/GreaterMetro/Boston/julia_ward_howe.html

Glossary

anonymously (uh NON uh muhss lee) Doing something without giving one's name.

governesses (GUH vur nuhss uhz) Women who teach and train children especially in a private home.

honeymoon (HUHN ee moon) A trip that a bride and groom take after their wedding day.

inheritance (in HAIR it uhnss) Money, property, or other items received from someone who has died.

patriotic (PAY tree AW tik) Doing something out of love of one's country.

rallying cry (RAL ee ing KRYE) A phrase used to get support for a cause.

reconciled (REK uhn siled) Became friendly again.

suffrage (SUHF rij) The right to vote.

Union (YOON yuhn) Another name for the United States of America during the Civil War.

vintage (VIN tij) Wine that is produced during a particular year.

— 9 —

Sarah Elizabeth Doyle: Champion for Women's Education

By Cheryl Kirk Noll

Sarah hurried past a rumbling horse-drawn streetcar. It was 1843, just days before her thirteenth birthday. She was starting at a brand new school. Providence High School was the first public high school in Rhode Island. It even had classes for girls.

Sarah climbed a steep hill. She walked through the Girls' entrance. It was her first step towards a lifetime **dedicated** to education for girls in Rhode Island.

....

Sarah Elizabeth Doyle was born in Providence, Rhode Island. She was the third of seven children.

When Sarah graduated from Providence High School, she became a teacher. After working in private schools, Sarah returned to her **alma mater**. She taught girls there for many years. Later, she became principal of the Girls' Department.

Sarah wore long skirts of gray or black. She pulled her hair into a tight bun. A small black bonnet often perched on her head. She may have looked prim and proper, but her students **idolized** her.

One said, "She walked with a swinging stride. She even looked **dynamic** when she was standing still."

Another said, "She was not only our teacher but the individual friend of each."

Sarah thought that women needed to "band together" in a world of men. She became President of the newly founded Rhode Island Women's Club. The club invited speakers to tea. They worked to improve themselves and society.

Many of the club's members were on a committee that had raised money for a women's exhibit at the 1876 **Centennial** Exposition in Philadelphia. Afterwards, they had $1,675 left over.

The committee voted to use the money to start a school to "aid in the **cultivation** of the arts of design." The small school they began was **co-educational**. Sarah was a founding member. She was secretary of the **Board of Trustees** for twenty-two years. Today, Rhode Island School of Design (RISD) is one of the best-known art schools in the world.

Sarah was 62 when she retired from Providence High School. But she kept working for educational rights for girls for the next thirty years.

Sarah wanted her students to be able to attend college. Brown College was in Providence. But it only accepted males. Sarah and other women urged Brown to accept women. Finally, in 1891, a new President quietly registered seven

TIDBITS

When Sarah was young, less than half of American children went to school. Those that did often attended private schools. Few went to high school, and most of these were boys from wealthy families.

Sarah was 22 when Rhode Island's neighbor, Massachusetts, became the first state to require school attendance. The law said children ages 8 to 14 should go to school for three months of the year female students for classes. Five years later, the Women's College at Brown University became official. It was the first college for women in Rhode Island. But the women were crowded into a small rented building. President Andrews of Brown asked Sarah to help create a permanent home for them.

Once again, Sarah invited a group of ladies to tea. They formed a new club. Sarah was president. Sarah threw herself into a year of raising money. Even schoolgirls proudly presented Miss Doyle with money. The club raised enough to build stately Pembroke Hall.

Miss Doyle gave a speech at the dedication ceremony in 1897. She said,

"Today marks an era in the education of women in [Rhode Island]. No longer need they stand at the door of the temple of knowledge, but [they] may enter."

Pembroke Hall as it looked in 1906.

TIDBITS

Sarah Doyle named Pembroke Hall. The founder of RI, Roger Williams, had studied at Pembroke College in England. A woman, the Countess de St. Pol, founded it in 1347.

The Women's College at Brown University was renamed Pembroke College in 1928. It merged with Brown University in 1971. Today the hall is the Pembroke Center for Teaching and Research on Women.

Timeline: Sarah Elizabeth Doyle

1830 ➤ March 23, Sarah Elizabeth Doyle is born to Thomas and Martha Doyle in Providence, RI.

1843 ➤ Sarah is a pupil in the first class of the Girls' Department at Providence High School. She graduates in 1846.

1846–1856 ➤ Sarah teaches at private schools.

1856–1878 ➤ She teaches in the Girls' Department at Providence High School.

1876–1884 ➤ Sarah is President of the Federation of Women's Clubs of RI.

1877–1899 ➤ She is on the Board of Trustees at Rhode Island School of Design.

1878–1892 ➤ Sarah is principal of the Girls' Department of Providence High School.

1884 ➤ She is the first woman to preside at a session of the National Education Association.

1889 ➤ She is a member of a committee appointed to draft a constitution for the General Federation of Women's Clubs.

1894 ➤ Sarah receives an honorary degree (M.A.) from Brown University.

The Sarah E. Doyle Club is formed to serve teachers in Providence. Many of its members are Sarah's former students.

1896 ➤ Sarah begins the RI Society for the Collegiate Education of Women (RISCEW). She serves as president until 1919.

1897 ➤ Pembroke Hall is erected with $38,000 raised by RISCEW.

1899–1903 ➤ Sarah is director of the Providence Athenaeum, a private library.

1906 ➤ She travels as a clubwoman to Naples, Italy.

1922 ➤ December 21, Sarah E. Doyle dies in Providence, Rhode Island. She is 92.

1971 ➤ Pembroke College merges with Brown University.

1974 ➤ The Sarah Doyle Women's Center is founded at Brown to support students around issues of **gender**. It houses an art gallery.

2008 ➤ Pembroke Hall is renovated and rededicated. It is home to the Pembroke Center for Teaching and Research on Women.

Learn More About Sarah Doyle and Education During Her Lifetime

- Bolden, Tonya, editor. ***33 Things Every Girl Should Know about Women's History: from Suffragettes to Skirt Lengths to the E.R.A.*** Crown Publishers, 2002.
- Colman, Penny. ***Girls: A History of Growing Up Female in America***. Scholastic, 2000.
- Nelson, Robin. ***School Then and Now***. Lerner Publications Co., 2003.

Web sites:

- Learn more about the Rhode Island School of Design with this video: http://www.risdmuseum.org/
- A short biography of Sarah Elizabeth Doyle: http://www.brown.edu/campus-life/support/sarah-doyle-center/guiding-philosophies/who-was-sarah-doyle

Glossary

alma mater (AWL muh MAW tur) A Latin term for the school one attended.

Board of Trustees (BORD uhv truhss TEEZ) A group of people who run an organization or business.

centennial (sen TEN ee uhl) The 100th year celebration of an event.

co-educational (KOH ej uh KAY shuhn uhl) A type of school that teaches both boys and girls.

cultivation (KUHL tuh vay shuhn) In this story, helping to develop knowledge by practice and study.

dedicated (DED uh KAY tuhd) Giving time and energy to a cause or a project.

dynamic (dye NAM ik) Filled with energy.

gender (JEN dur) The sex of a person or an animal.

idolized (EYE duhl ized) Loved, adored.

—10—

Ida Lewis: Lighthouse Keeper, American Heroine

by Sally P. Riley

Sixteen-year-old Ida looked out the window of the Lime Rock lighthouse where she lived. A boat with four boys was sailing in Newport Harbor. She watched one boy climb the mast and rock back and forth. Was he trying to scare his friends? Suddenly the boat **capsized**, and the boys fell into the water. They struggled to keep their heads above the waves. Ida ran to her rowboat and headed toward the boys. Would she get there in time?

Idawalley Zoradia Lewis was born in February 1842 in Newport, Rhode Island. Ida loved the sea. She was happy when her father, Hosea Lewis became lighthouse keeper of the Lime Rock Light Station in Newport Harbor. Ida was eleven.

This lighthouse sat on a small island made of **limestone**. It was 1/8 of a mile from the mainland. Twice a day, Hosea rowed to the lighthouse to tend the lantern. Sometimes, if the weather was calm, he took Ida with him. He let her row the boat. If the weather was stormy, Hosea went alone. He stayed in a one-room shack on the island. After almost four years, Congress approved money to build a house. The Lewis family moved into their new home in 1857. Ida loved living on Lime Rock.

Four months after moving in, Hosea suffered a crippling stroke. Ida left school to help her mother tend the lighthouse and care for her father. Every day she rowed her two younger brothers and her younger sister to the mainland for school and bought supplies in Newport. Stormy weather never stopped Ida from making these trips.

By fourteen, Ida was known as the best swimmer in Newport. Many times, she used her swimming and rowing skills to save lives. Her first rescue, at only sixteen, was when she saved the four boys in Newport Harbor. They were embarrassed, and told no one what Ida had done.

Eleven years later, Ida was sitting by the fire on a stormy night. She was sick with a cold. Her mother saw an overturned boat with men in the water beside it. She called to Ida. Ida didn't take time to put on shoes or a coat. She ran to her boat and struggled to row to the men. The rain and wind were terrible and the waves were high. Ida pulled the two men into her boat and brought them back to the island. They were so grateful that they told everyone about the rescue. Ida's quiet life changed forever. She was no longer just a lighthouse keeper's daughter. Now she had become the heroine of Lime Rock. As many as 9,000 people visited the island that summer. July 4, 1869 was declared Ida Lewis Day.

TIDBITS

Ida was only 5 feet 4 inches tall and weighed 103 pounds. She performed her daring rescues wearing long dresses.

On Ida Lewis Day, Ida received a new **mahogany** boat. The *Rescue* had velvet cushions and gold-filled **oarlocks**. But she always used her small old rowboat for her rescues.

President Ulysses S. Grant visited Ida. He said, "I am happy to meet you, Ida Lewis, as one of the heroic, noble women of the age."

TIDBITS

In 1907, Ida wrote: "Sometimes … the waves are so high that no boat would dare come near the rock, not even if we were starving. But I am happy. There's a peace on this rock that you don't get on shore. There are hundreds of boats going in and out of this harbor in summer, and it's part of my happiness to know that they are depending on me to guide them safely."

After her father died in 1872, Ida hoped she would be named the lighthouse keeper. Usually no **appointment** was made, and women **succeeded** their husbands. No woman had ever been officially named a keeper. Seven years later, though, Ida received an official appointment and replaced her mother.

Documented records say Ida saved eighteen lives. But people talked about many more. Ida never kept count because she felt she was only doing her job.

Ida's last rescue occurred when she was 64 years old. She died of a stroke in 1911 at the age of 69. She was still tending the Lime Rock Lighthouse.

No one knows the exact number of lives Ida Lewis saved.

Timeline: Ida Lewis

1842 ➤ February 25, Idawalley Zoradia Lewis is born to Hosea Lewis and Idawalley Zoradia Wiley Lewis. She is the second of 5 children.

1853 ➤ November 5, Hosea Lewis is appointed keeper of Lime Rock Light.

1857 ➤ June 29, the Lewis family moves into a new home on Lime Rock.

August, Hosea suffers a paralyzing stroke.

1858 ➤ September 4, Ida rescues four boys whose boat capsized in Newport Harbor.

1866 ➤ February, Ida rescues a drunken sailor who has stolen Ida's brother Rudolph's boat to row back to Fort Adams. Ida is unable to save the boat.

1867 ➤ January, Ida rescues two men who have stolen Rudolph's replacement boat to catch a prized sheep that jumped into the harbor and is being taken out to sea. After saving the two men, Ida saves the sheep.

1869 ➤ Ida rescues two soldiers whose boat capsized near the channel to the open ocean. The publicity which follows makes Ida a national heroine.

July 4, Newport celebrates Ida Lewis Day with a parade and speeches.

Summer, thousands of people visit Ida, including President Ulysses S. Grant and Vice President Schuyler Colfax.

1872 ➤ November 17, Ida's father dies and her mother succeeds him as the unofficial keeper of the Lime Rock Lighthouse.

1879 ➤ January 21, Ida is finally officially named keeper of Lime Rock.

1881 ➤ Ida rescues two Fort Adams soldiers who have fallen through the ice. She is awarded the Gold Lifesaving Medal by the US Lifesaving Service – the first woman to receive this honor.

1906 ➤ Ida, who is now 64 years old, rescues a friend who is rowing to Lime Rock for a visit.

1911 ➤ October 21, Ida suffers a stroke shortly after putting out the Lime Rock lantern.

October 24, Ida dies, and all the harbor boats toll their bells.

1924 ➤ February, the RI state legislature votes to change the name of Lime Rock Light to Ida Lewis Rock Light. This is the first time a lighthouse has been named for its keeper.

Learn More About Ida Lewis and Lighthouses

- Licameli, Doris. ***Rowing to the Rescue: The Story of Ida Lewis, Famous Lighthouse Heroine.*** Lulu Enterprises, 2006.
- Skomal, Lenore. ***The Lighthouse Keeper's Daughter: The Remarkable True Story of American Heroine Ida Lewis.*** GPP, 2010.

Web sites:

- Information and pictures of Ida Lewis and Lime Rock Lighthouse: http://lighthouse.cc/limerock/history.html
- Information about lighthouse keeping: http://www.nps.gov/history/maritime/keep/keephero.htm
- Photographs and histories of all lighthouses in the United States and many in Canada: http://www.lighthousefriends.com/

Glossary

appointment (uh POINT muhnt) In this story, the act of naming someone to take over a particular job or position.

capsized (KAP sized) Something such as a boat that has turned over in the water.

documented (DOK yuh MUHNT uhd) Keeping track of an event by writing down the facts, taking pictures, or filming the event.

limestone (LIME stohn) A hard rock that has been formed by crushed shells or coral. It is used for building or for making cement.

mahogany (muh HOG uh nee) Very strong, reddish brown wood that comes from a tree that grows in tropical forests. The wood often is used to make furniture.

oarlocks (OR lokss) Curved pieces of metal that are attached to the sides of a rowboat. They help to keep the boat's oars attached.

succeeded (suhk SEED uhd) Managed to do or finish something.

—11—

Annie Smith Peck: Mountain Climber

by Deborah Bruss

Annie hoped it would only take two hours to reach the peak of Mount Illampu. The mountain guide told her not to proceed. But Annie couldn't quit now. Her goal was to climb higher than any man or women in the Americas.

A thin layer of snow covered the steep, icy incline. Annie took the lead, using her ice ax to help pull herself forward. A safety rope tied her to the mountain guide and a porter. She poked with the ax handle, feeling for solid footing. Without warning, the handle went in deep. Annie looked through the hole it left and into a deep **crevasse**. She turned around to ask for help. "…I saw to my horror and disgust the rope trailing idly on the snow…." The two men had untied the rope and refused to follow.

Annie Smith Peck was born in 1850 into a wealthy family in Providence, Rhode Island. She tried to keep up with her older brothers. Perhaps this desire taught her to be tough and **persevere**. After college, she became a teacher, and then traveled to Europe.

On a train ride through the Swiss Alps, Annie saw a jagged, icy mountain. It was the **infamous** Matterhorn. Many men had fallen to their death trying to conquer it. But Annie was awed and vowed to climb it.

Annie returned to Switzerland in 1895. She became the third woman to climb the Matterhorn. Many people were shocked because she had worn pants, not a skirt.

In 1897, Annie climbed the highest mountain in Mexico – snowcapped Citlaltépetl (18,700 feet). She set the women's altitude record. Next she climbed a 17,887-foot active volcano near Mexico City. But this mountain wasn't challenging enough.

Annie wanted to climb Illampu (20,873 feet) in the **Andes**. No one had ever climbed it. She found it hard to raise funds for her expeditions. Most people thought she was foolish, or even insane. After five years of planning, Annie left New York for Bolivia. Two mountain guides and a geology professor accompanied her. It took five weeks to reach the base of Illampu. The professor got **altitude sickness.** The porters couldn't hike on snow and glaciers because they wore sandals. Annie had to turn back. She tried again in 1904. When she neared the summit, her guide refused to follow.

Annie headed to Mt. Huascarán (21,812 feet) in Peru. She made five attempts over the next five years. Usually she hired European mountain guides. Once she hired a charming Peruvian. People said he was "**loco**." She hired him anyways.

TIDBITS

"I decided in my teens that I would ... show that women had as much brains as men and could do things as well if she gave them her undivided attention."

In Peru, Annie sewed long underwear for the porters who carried the gear. The only color she could find was pink.

Annie was a **suffragette**. In 1911, she planted a *Votes for Women* banner on Mount Coropuna (21,074 feet) in Peru.

The climb was a disaster. Valuable equipment was lost. The "loco" told the porters to strike for more pay. Later, Annie heard that the "loco" thought of murdering her.

At age 58, when most women were grandmothers, Annie finally reached the summit. She is the only woman to be the first to climb a major world peak. The seven-hour descent was "a horrible nightmare." It was dark, frigid and windy. Annie slipped and slid. One guide's strong grip on the rope saved their lives. The other guide dropped Annie's mitten and then his own. They both got frostbite. Annie's hand recovered but part of the guide's hand and foot had to be **amputated**.

When she was 80, Annie set out to fly all the commercial routes in South America. At 84, Annie climbed her last mountain – Mount Madison (5774 feet) in New Hampshire.

Annie Peck and two guides.

TIDBITS

On Mount Huascarán, Annie's guide lost her warm Eskimo suit, so she wore 2 pairs of tights, 3 wool suits of long underwear, canvas **knicker-bockers**, 2 shirts, a jacket, 2 sweaters and 4 pairs of wool socks. But all this clothing didn't protect her from the wind.

A young American struggled up a glacier after Annie. He said she was, "… neither a man nor a woman; she is a cat."

Timeline: Annie Smith Peck

1850 ➤ October 19, Annie Peck is born in Providence, Rhode Island to George and Ann Power Smith Peck. She has three older brothers.

1850–1872 ➤ Annie grows up in Providence. She attends Dr. Stockbridge's School for Young Ladies, Providence High School and the R.I. State Normal School.

1877–1884 ➤ At the University of Michigan, Annie gets her master's degree in Greek. She becomes one of America's first women college professors.

1884–1985 ➤ She studies music in Germany and is the first woman to attend the American School of **Classical Studies** in Athens, Greece.

1886–1895 ➤ Back in the US, Annie teaches at Smith College, heads west to climb mountains, and gives lectures on Greek and Roman Archaeology.

1895 ➤ At 45, Annie becomes the third woman to climb the Matterhorn (14,691 feet).

1897 ➤ Mexico is next. She climbs Citlaltépetl (in English - Mount Orizaba) and the volcano Popocateptl (in English - El Popo).

1903 ➤ Annie hires two Swiss mountain guides and heads to Bolivia. They don't make it to the top of Illampu (in English - Sonata). Annie returns to the U.S.

1904 ➤ Annie hires an Austrian mountain guide for her second attempt on Illampu. She doesn't trust him after he unties the safety rope. She does not reach the top.

Twice, Annie attempts to find a route up Mt. Huascarán. Native Indian porters do not have proper clothing for the frigid temperatures, fierce snowstorms and high winds.

1906–1908 ➤ Annie attempts Mt. Huascarán three more times. Then on the fourth, she makes it. No man or woman had ever climbed this high in the Americas.

1911 ➤ Annie writes about her famous climbs in *A Search for the Apex of America*.

1928 ➤ The Peruvian government names Huascarán's north peak, *Cumbre Aña Peck*.

1932 ➤ Annie publishes, *Flying Over South America: Twenty Thousand Miles by Air*.

1935 ➤ July 18, at age 84, Annie Peck Smith dies of pneumonia in New York City.

Learn More About Annie Smith Peck and Mountain Climbing

- Devine, Monica. ***Mountain Climbing: Scaling the Heights.*** Perfection Learning Corporation, 1997.
- ***Women Explorers (Junior Edition): 100 Years of Mountain Adventure.*** Altitude Publishing, 2006.

Web sites:

- A short biography of Annie Smith Peck: http://www.ric.edu/faculty/rpotter/smithpeck.html
- Annie Smith Peck reaches the summit of Peru's Mount Huascaran: http://www.loe.org/series/discovery_women/peck.php
- Read about Mt. Denali, the highest mountain in North America: http://pbskids.org/nova/denali/

Glossary

altitude sickness (AL ti tood SIK ness) An illness caused when mountain climbers experience reduced air pressure and lower oxygen levels as they climb higher. The illness causes headache, fast heart rates, shortness of breath, confusion, fatigue, and sometimes, coughing up blood.

amputated (AM pyuh TAY tuhd) Cuttting off a person's arm, leg, toe, or finger because it is injured and will not heal. Doctors amputate to stop the damaged limb from infecting other parts of a body.

Andes (AN deez) A mountain range on the western side of South America.

classical studies (KLASS uh kuhl STUHD eez) The study of Ancient Greece and Ancient Rome.

crevasse (cruh VAHSS) A deep, jagged cut or hole in a glacier.

infamous (IN fuh muhss) Having a bad reputation.

knickerbockers (NIK ur baw kurz) Short pants that end just below the knee. Also called knickers.

loco (LOH coh) Crazy.

persevere (pur suh VEER) To keep trying even though there are difficulties.

suffragette (suhf rij ET) Name given to a woman who works for the right to vote.

—12—

Alva Vanderbilt Belmont:

Socialite and Suffragette

by K. D. Huxman

Alva Smith Vanderbilt was tired of being snubbed by New York society. She used her new husband's wealth to build a beautiful mansion. Alva helped design it. Many thought it looked like a French castle. Everyone wanted to see what it looked like inside. To show off her new house, Alva threw a costume party. Alva decided to invite only her friends. Now everyone wanted to be her friend. Alva helped the Vanderbilt family climb to the top of New York society.

....

Alva Ertskin Smith was born in Mobile, Alabama in 1853. She was the second daughter in a family of nine children. Her father was in the cotton business. He and Alva's mother wanted to move up in the world. They wanted their daughters to marry well.

When Alva was still a young woman they moved to New York City. Alva and her sisters went to France to finish their schooling. Alva was twenty-one when she made her **debut** in New York society. She met William Kissam Vanderbilt. His friends called him Willie K. He asked

Alva to marry him. She said yes but they had to convince their families that it was a good choice. The Vanderbilt family was wealthier than Alva's family. But both families had little social status. The Vanderbilt's were rich but the family name was not respected. The Smith's were too new to New York to have society's regard. Alva and Willie won their families' blessings. They married later that year. It took longer for New York society to accept them.

Willie and Alva never had to worry about money. They had big, beautiful homes in New York City and Long Island, New York. Alva built another wonderful mansion in Newport, Rhode Island. She helped design it. She named the house Marble House. Many wealthy families spent the summer in Newport. Alva collected beautiful decorations for her homes. Today Marble house is a National Historic Landmark. The couple had three children. Alva worked hard to be a good wife and mother. But even with a life of riches she and Willie were not happy together.

Alva caused a **scandal** when she divorced Willie in 1895. She married Oliver Hazard Perry Belmont in 1896. Alva and Oliver had no children together. They had a happy marriage until he died in 1908.

After Oliver's death Alva threw herself into social causes. She became a **suffragette**. She devoted her time and money toward getting women the right to vote. She traveled to other countries to meet women who wanted to vote in their own countries. She opened her homes to meetings. Alva even

TIDBITS

The time in which Alva lived was called the **Gilded Age.** During the Gilded Age, New York society was ruled by the Four Hundred. These were families of wealth and power. Alva and Willie K. wanted to become friends with them. Alva's costume ball was the Vanderbilt's ticket into high society.

Mark Twain wrote a book titled *The Gilded Age*. It made fun of the **excesses** of the wealthy.

wrote an operetta about the cause. She had a Chinese tea house built near Marble House. Her Conference of Great Women was held there.

After years of work the Nineteenth Amendment to the U.S. Constitution was passed. On August 18, 1920, American women were finally granted the right to vote.

Alva continued to work for social causes. She supported labor unions and prisoner's rights. She became known as an expert in **architecture**, too. She spent her later years in France where she bought and restored a 15th century **chateau**. When Alva died, she was remembered as a tireless worker for others. She was a woman who used the vast resources available to her to make the world a better place.

Men and women leave Marble House after attending the Conference of Great Women in 1914.

TIDBITS

Alva was a good building designer. She was the only woman at the time elected a member of the American Institute of Architects.

The **operetta** Alva wrote about women's suffrage was called *Melinda and Her Sisters.*

Timeline: Alva Vanderbilt Belmont

1853 ➤ January 17, Alva Ertskin Smith is born in Mobile, Alabama. Her father, Murray Forbes Smith, is a cotton planter and merchant. Her mother is Phoebe Ann Smith.

Early 1870's ➤ The family moves to New York City. Alva and her sisters attend private school in France.

1875 ➤ On April 20, Alva marries William Kissam Vanderbilt.

1887 ➤ Alva and Willie's only daughter, Consuelo, is born.

1878 ➤ William Kissam, their first son, is born.

1881 ➤ Alva hires architect Richard Morris Hunt to design a mansion on 5th Avenue in New York City. It cost three million dollars and generated a lifelong love of architecture in Alva.

1884 ➤ Their second son and third child, Harold Stirling, is born.

1889 ➤ Alva hires Hunt to design a mansion in Newport, Rhode Island.

1892 ➤ Marble House, in Newport, Rhode Island, opens.

1893 ➤ Alva and Willie K. invite friends and neighbors to take a world cruise on their yacht. One of their neighbors is Oliver Hazard Perry Belmont, known as O.H.P. Alva decides to divorce Willie K.

1895 ➤ Alva's divorce from Willie K. is final.

1896 ➤ Alva marries O.H.P. Belmont. The mayor of New York City performs the ceremony.

1908 ➤ O.H.P. Belmont dies.

1919 ➤ On June 4, Congress passes the 19th amendment to the U.S. Constitution.

1920 ➤ Alva is elected president of the National Women's Party.

August 18, Congress **ratifies** the 19th amendment to the U.S. Constitution. Women are granted the right to vote.

After 1924 ➤ Alva lives in France.

1933 ➤ January 26, Alva Ertskin Smith Vanderbilt Belmont dies in Paris, France.

Learn More About Alva Vanderbilt Belmont, Suffragettes, and the Gilded Age

- Clark, Judith Freeman. ***The Gilded Age (Eyewitness History Series)***. Facts on File, 2006.
- McNeese, Tim. ***The Gilded Age and Progressivism 1891-1913 (Discovering U.S. History)***. Chelsea House, 2010.

Web sites:

- Alva and the National Woman's Party: http://memory.loc.gov/ammem/collections/suffrage/nwp/profiles2.html
- The 19th Amendment: http://www.ourdocuments.gov/doc.php?flash=true&doc=63

Glossary

architecture (AR ki tek chur) The act of designing buildings; the style of different buildings.

chateau (sha TOH) A castle or palace; also, a large second home built in the country.

debut (day BYOO) The first time a young woman enters society, usually on the night of a special party. A debut signaled that a young woman was ready for marriage.

excesses (EK sess uhz) Too much of something.

Gilded Age (GILD uhd AYJ) Displays of abundant wealth by America's upper class that happened from about 1865-1901.

operetta (OP uh RET uh) A musical play in which some of the lines are spoken and some are sung.

ratifies (RAT uh fyez) Officially agrees to something such as the passage of a bill in Congress.

scandal (SKAN duhl) Disgraceful or shocking behavior.

suffragette (suhf rij ET) Name given to a woman who worked for the right to vote.

— 13 —

Matilda Sissieretta Joyner Jones: Opera Singer

by Barbara J. Turner

Sissy stood on stage at Boston's Music Hall and stared out at the audience. Five-thousand people. She had never sung for such a large group before. Could she do it? Would she please them?

Sissy began to sing. It was what she was born to do. She sang and sang and when she stopped, the audience rose as one, cheering and clapping. The roar was overwhelming.

Tears of joy filled Sissy's eyes.

She was an opera singer. She was.

Matilda Sissieretta Joyner was born in Portsmouth, Virginia in 1869. Her family moved to Providence, Rhode Island when she was seven. Her father, Jeremiah Malachi Joyner, became Pastor of the Pond Street Church. Her mother, Henrietta Beale, was a homemaker and sang in the church choir. Just five years before Sissy's birth, they had been slaves.

Sissy loved to sing. She sang at church and school. Her parents encouraged her. At fourteen, she enrolled in the Providence Academy of

TIDBITS

When Sissy toured across America, she traveled in a $30,000 private railroad car.

At the height of her fame, Sissy earned $2,000 for a week's performance. She was the highest paid African-American singer of her time. Adelina Patti, the white soprano, received $4,000 for a single performance.

Sissy acquired many medals throughout her career and always wore them across her chest at performances.

Music. That same year, she met David Richard Jones. He was a hotel **bellman**. They married and he became her manager.

Sissy sang all kinds of music, but she loved opera best. She dreamed of singing on stage in an opera. She went to the New England Conservatory of Music to learn more. Two years later, she made her professional **debut** at Wallack's Theater in New York.

The audience loved her. Sissy reached all the high notes and all the low ones, too. Her **range** was unbelievable. People called her the 'Black Patti' after the Italian **soprano,** Adelina Patti.

A **musical director** heard Sissy sing. He **telegraphed** a **theatrical manager** he knew. They booked her for a tour of the West Indies. Sissy toured for eight months. She was given gold, jewels and medals for her many performances. Back in America, she toured all the big cities. She sang at **Expositions** and in music halls. She even sang for President Harrison at the White House. Then she sang at the Grand Negro Jubilee at Madison Square Garden. The performance made her famous.

Now people talked about her starring in an opera at the Metropolitan Opera House in New York. Sissy was thrilled. This was her dream. It was what she had worked for. But it never happened. It was one thing for African-Americans to sing and dance for white people. But to be given a starring role in an opera? It just wasn't done.

Sissy was hurt and disappointed, but she didn't stop singing. She toured Europe where her color didn't matter.

She sang for kings and queens and princes. She sang for the **Kaiser.** None of them cared about her color. They cared about her voice.

Sissy returned to America. She knew there were many places where she would never be allowed to sing. She formed her own group of jugglers, singers, dancers and comedians. She called it the Black Patti **Troubadours.** They performed all over America for people who appreciated their talents. At the end of every show, Sissy always sang a few pieces from operas.

The Troubadours toured for twenty years before breaking up. Sissy returned to Rhode Island. She spent the rest of her life caring for her mother and took in two homeless children. She also gave much of her time to her church. She died of cancer on June 24, 1933.

A poster advertising Madame Sissieretta Jones.

TIDBITS

Sissy did not like being called the 'Black Patti.' She preferred Madame Jones. Still, she used it in the Black Patti Troubadours because everyone recognized that name.

While touring with the Troubadours, Sissy discovered she was almost broke. Her husband had squandered away most of their money. When she retired, she had to sell her homes and jewels to make ends meet. She died penniless.

Timeline: Matilda Sissieretta Joyner Jones

1869 ➤	January 5, Sissy is born in Portsmouth, Virginia to Jeremiah Malachi Joyner and Henrietta Beale.
1876 ➤	The Joyners move to Providence, Rhode Island, hoping for better economic and educational opportunities.
1883 ➤	Sissy studies music at the Providence Academy of Music with Ada Baroness Lacombe.
	She marries David Richard Jones, a hotel bellman.
1887 ➤	Sissy sings for an audience of 5,000 at a fund-raising concert for the Parnell Defense Fund.
	She studies at the New England Conservatory of Music with Flora Batson.
1888 ➤	June 13, Sissy makes her professional debut at Wallack's Theater in New York.
1890 ➤	Sissy tours the West Indies.
1892 ➤	April, Sissy sings at the three-day Grand Negro Jubilee at Madison Square Garden and becomes a celebrity.
	She signs a three year contract with Major J. B. Pond, manager of Mark Twain and Reverend Henry Ward Beecher.
	She becomes the highest paid African-American singer up to that time.
1893 ➤	Sissy performs at the Columbia World Exposition in Chicago.
	She sings and tours with Gilmore's Band.
1894 ➤	Sissy sings for President Harrison in the White House Blue Room.
	She performs at the Buffalo Exposition and the Pittsburgh Exposition.
	She performs at the Wintergarden Theater in Berlin.
1895 ➤	Sissy forms the Black Patti Troubadours and tours America for twenty years.
1898 ➤	Sissy learns her husband is squandering her money and files for divorce.
1916 ➤	The Black Patti Troubadours disband. Sissy retires to care for her aging mother. She takes in two homeless children and contributes much time to her church.
1933 ➤	June 24, Matilda Sissieretta Joyner Jones dies of cancer in Rhode Island.

Learn More About Matilda Sissieretta Joyner Jones and the Opera

- O'Donnell, Jessica. ***Leontyne Price: First Lady of Opera.*** Gareth Stevens Publishing, 2010.
- Siberell, Anne. ***Bravo! Brava! A Night at the Opera: Behind the Scenes with Composers, Cast and Crew.*** Oxford University press, 2002.

Web sites:

- Women in History-Sissieretta Jones: http://www.lkwdpl.org/wihohio/jone-sis.htm
- Black History Pages-Sissieretta Jones: http://www.blackhistorypages.net/pages/sjones.php

Glossary

bellman (BEL muhn) A person who works for a hotel, and is hired to carry luggage and do errands.

debut (day BYOO) In this story, a first-time performance of a dance or show.

expositions (ek SPUH zi shuhnz) Large fairs or public exhibits.

Kaiser (KEYE zur) An emperor. The title given to the rulers of Austria or Germany until 1918.

musical director(MYOO zuh kuhl duh REK tur) The person who leads a music group or play performed with songs.

range (RAYNJ) In this story, the difference between the highest and lowest notes of a voice or instrument.

soprano (suh PRAN oh) The highest singing voice. A person who sings in a soprano voice.

telegraphed (TEL uh graft) Sent a message over a long distance using a machine that sends code over a wire.

theatrical manager (thee AT ruh kuhl MAN uh jur) A person who is in charge of organizing the lights, sound, scenery, and props in a play.

troubadours (TROO buh dorz) Singers, poets, or other performers who traveled around the castles of Europe in the 1100s and 1200s.

—14—

Nancy Elizabeth Prophet: African - American Sculptor

by K. D. Huxman

Nancy Elizabeth Prophet had both American Indian and African American ancestors. She knew that **racism** would make an art career difficult. Racism kept many black people from making the most of their talents. After Nancy finished art school her work was chosen for a local **exhibition**. She was told to stay away from the opening. People of color were not invited.

Nancy decided to go to Paris, France. Other African American artists had done well there. She hoped her mixed race and artistic gifts would be accepted there, too.

Nancy was born in 1890. She grew up in Warwick, Rhode Island. Her father was a laborer. Her mother was a housewife and cook. Nancy was always interested in art. Her parents saw no value in art as a career. Nancy worked as a **domestic** as a teenager. The work made her aware of how hard it would be, as a woman of color, to follow her dreams.

Nancy was accepted into the Rhode Island School of Design (RISD).

She majored in drawing and painting. Some of her best pieces were portraits. In her second year at RISD she married Francis Ford. Francis was a student at Brown University. Their marriage was not a happy one.

Nancy was the first African American to graduate from RISD. She tried to make a living by doing portraits. She found that her art was welcome but she was not. Nancy saved the money she earned as a domestic to go to France. She arrived in Paris, France several years later. She worked hard. She took up sculpting. Money was always a problem. She only had $380.00 when she arrived in France. For a while she was so poor that she lived on orange marmalade and tea for two months. Nancy became so discouraged that she destroyed a sculpture she spent three months making. She had to rely on the kindness of **patrons of the arts** for help.

Her work was praised by many critics in France and in the United States. Her impressive sculptures were shown in both countries. *Congolaise*, a **bust** of an African man sculpted from cherry wood is considered Nancy's very best work.

In 1934 Nancy accepted a teaching position at Spelman College in Atlanta, Georgia. She taught there for ten years. She did not have to worry about money but she had less time to sculpt. Nancy's students thought she was a tough but fair teacher. Nancy liked to dress differently. She walked around the campus with a cape flapping around her. Many of her students thought she was **eccentric**.

Nancy went back to Rhode Island in 1944. She worked

TIDBITS

Soon after graduating from RISD Nancy changed the spelling of her last name from Profitt to Prophet. She might have done this to separate herself from her parents who disapproved of her being an artist.

Silence, Nancy's first known sculpture, was completed during her first year in France.

Nancy did sculptures in many materials. She used marble, wood, bronze, **alabaster**, granite, **terracotta**, clay and plaster.

in a ceramics factory for a short time. Her father was ill. She cared for him. To earn money she worked as a domestic again. Her glory days as an artist were over. Even though she died in **obscurity** in 1960, she left a legacy of art. She will always be remembered as a talented sculptor who made a lasting contribution to the world.

TIDBITS

In the years when Nancy was a young woman there was a lot of pressure for women to marry and have children. Nancy chose her own path when she decided to be an artist.

Nancy was close friends with the African American writer, W.E.B. DuBois. DuBois helped create the National Association for the Advancement of Colored People (NAACP) in 1909.

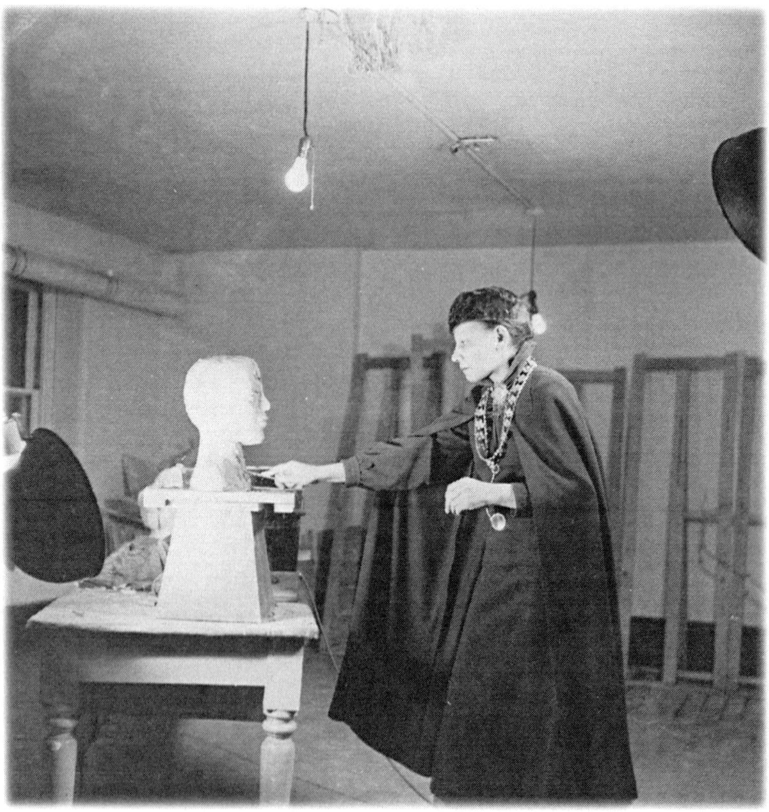

Nancy Prophet teaching sculpting.

Timeline: Nancy Elizabeth Prophet

1890 ➤ March 19, Nancy Elizabeth is born to William H. Profitt and Rosa E. Walker Profitt in Warwick, Rhode Island.

1914 ➤ Nancy is admitted to the Rhode Island School of Design (RISD).

1915 ➤ On January 30, Nancy marries Francis Ford, a man ten years older than she. He attends Brown University but never graduates. They often live apart. They have no children.

1918 ➤ Nancy graduates from RISD with a degree in painting and freehand drawing. She is the first African-American to graduate from RISD.

1922 ➤ Nancy travels to Paris, France to live and work.

1924 ➤ One of Nancy's wooden busts is included in the *Salon D'Automne* exhibition in Paris.

1925-1927 ➤ Nancy's works are included in the *Salon D'Automne* exhibitions and shipped to exhibitions at RISD and in Boston, Massachusetts.

1927 ➤ The Students Fund of Boston starts sending Nancy $30 per month to help her pay her way.

1929 ➤ Nancy visits the United States for eleven months but returns to France.

Early 1930's ➤ Patrons of the Arts, Edouard and Julia Champion, support Nancy by paying her rent and buying her meals

1932 ➤ Two of Nancy's sculptures are exhibited in Paris, France. Critics praise her work.

Nancy visits the United States where she exhibits in Boston. She is elected a member of the Art Association of Newport, Rhode Island.

1933 ➤ Nancy returns to Paris, France, but again has difficulty paying her debts.

1934 ➤ Nancy accepts a teaching position at Spelman College in Atlanta, Georgia.

1944 ➤ After ten years, Nancy leaves Spelman College and moves to Providence, Rhode Island. She works as a domestic.

1960 ➤ December 18, Nancy Elizabeth Prophet dies of a heart attack in Providence, Rhode Island.

1978 ➤ Nancy's pieces are part of the "Four from Providence" exhibit at the Bannister Gallery of Rhode Island College.

Learn More about Nancy Elizabeth Prophet and Sculpting

- Burby, Liza N. ***A Day in the Life of a Sculptor***. The Rosen Publishing Group, Inc. 1999.
- Hanson, Anders. ***Cool Sculpture: the Art of Creativity for Kids***. ABDO Pub., 2009.

Web sites:

- Two short biographies of Nancy Elizabeth Prophet:
  http://www.aaregistry.org/historic_events/view/nancy-elizabeth-prophet-unknown-sculptor
  http://www.atlantaintownpaper.com/features/SpelmanMuseumFEB07.php

Glossary

alabaster (AL uh bass tur) A smooth, white, type of stone.
bust (BUHST) A sculpture that shows a person's head and shoulders.
domestic (duh MESS tik) In this story, a maid. Someone who keeps a house clean.
eccentric (ek SEN trik) Acting in an odd or strange but not threatening way.
exhibition (ek suh BISH uhn) A public showing of art, skills, or historical objects.
obscurity (uhb SKYOOR uh tee) Without being known or understood.
patrons of the arts (PAY truhnz of the ARTSS) Wealthy people who give money to pay the bills of artists in order to allow the artists to create new works.
racism (RAY siz uhm) Treating people of other races as if they were inferior.
terra-cotta (TER uh KOT uh) A type of hard, red-brown clay used to make pottery, sculptures, and roof tiles.

— 15 —

Princess Red Wing: Speaker for Her Tribe

by Linda Crotta Brennan

Princess Red Wing and Eva Butler painted the building. They set out birch bark baskets. They hung strings of **wampum**. They placed peace pipes in display cases. They labeled each item. Outside they planted a circle of evergreens. Finally, their Tomaquag Museum was ready.

Later, four hundred people gathered outside in the friendship circle. In a special ceremony, corn, beans, and squash were planted.

Princess Red Wing wore a beaded head band and a deer skin dress. Her silver bracelets jangled as she motioned a couple forward. They presented their baby for his naming ceremony.

Princess Red Wing was born in 1896 in Connecticut. Her legal name was Mary Ella Glasko. Her native name was Red Wing. She was a **Narragansett** and **Wampanoag** Indian.

Red Wing's ancestor was Metacomet. He was chief of the

TIDBITS

In the 1600s fighting broke out between the Southern New England tribes and the English colonists. Princess Red Wing's ancestor, Metacomet, was chief of the Wampanoags at the time. The war was named King Philip's War after him.

In 1945, the New England Council of Indian Chiefs gave Princess Red Wing the title Squaw Sachem. This title meant she was a leader of her people.

Wampanoags in the 1600s. Europeans called him King Philip. Red Wing went by the title "Princess."

When she was little, Red Wing's family moved to Rhode Island. There were seven children. Still, her mother always used a white tablecloth at meal times. She said her children's manners should be good enough for the president.

After high school, Red Wing went to teacher training school. Then she studied art in New York City. She wanted to share her native **culture**. Red Wing became a teacher. She worked in summer camps. She visited schools.

Red Wing married Horace Peek. They had one son, Walter. Her husband died when Red Wing was 31. Later, she married Mohawk chief Daniel Congdon. His native name was White Oak. They had a daughter Susan (native name Bear Flower). They had a son Thomas (native name Metacomet).

Princess Red Wing worked to strengthen her tribe. She helped write the rules of the Narragansetts. She designed the tribe's **official seal**. She edited *The Narragansett Dawn.* This magazine allowed the tribe to share news, stories, and poems. It also taught Narragansett vocabulary words.

Princess Red Wing helped organize **powwows** around Rhode Island. The games, music, dancing, and storytelling brought the tribe together. Non-natives also were invited.

Historian Eva Lutz Butler was Princess Red Wing's friend. Eva had a large collection of Native American **artifacts**. Together, they established the Tomaquag Indian Memorial Museum. It focused on the Narragansetts. It also included other tribes of Southern New England.

After Eva died, Princess Red Wing ran the museum. She moved it to a new building. In a classroom next door, she taught "the lovely things of Indianhood."

Princess Red Wing was a talented writer, too. She wrote poetry, plays, songs, and a newspaper column. She created prayers and pageants. She wrote down legends. Some of her work won awards.

Princess Red Wing traveled all over the country to speak. She also gave talks in Canada, England, and Amsterdam. She served on a committee for the United Nations. She met with world leaders. She dined with First Lady Eleanor Roosevelt.

In 1978, Princess Red Wing was named Rhode Island's Woman of the Year. The governor declared June 23, 1978 Princess Red Wing Day.

When she got older, Princess Red Wing moved in with friends. They lived next to her beloved Tomaquag Museum. The friends owned an Indian restaurant named Dovecrest. Princess Red Wing read tea leaves there. She continued sharing her native culture until her death in 1987 at age 92.

The Tomaquag Indian Memorial Museum as it appeared when the Dovecrest Restaurant was open.

TIDBITS

Red Wing's full title was Princess Red Wing of the Seven Crescents of the Royal House of Pokanoket, Narragansett Tribe, Wampanoag Nation.

Red Wing wrote a poem about being a red wing blackbird flinging *A message red and burning to ears… For the purpose, of the uplift of my race.*

The Dovecrest Restaurant served Native American food like johnnycakes, **succotash**, Indian pudding, seafood, wild game and strawberry bread.

Timeline: Princess Red Wing

1896	March 21, Mary Ella Glasko is born to Walter and Hannah Glasko in Connecticut. In her Indian naming ceremony, she is given the name Red Wing.
1914	Red Wing graduates from Burrillville High School.
1916	She graduates from Teacher's Training School.
1927	Red Wing's first husband, Horace Peek, dies.
1934	She helps draft the bylaws for Narragansett Indian Tribe.
1936	Red Wing marries Daniel Congdon, a Mohawk chief.
1934–37	She serves as the editor of *The Narragansett Dawn.*
1947–1970	Princess Red Wing serves as a member of the Speaker's Research Committee of the **Undersecretariat** for the United Nations.
1958	Princess Red Wing and Eva Lutz Butler open the Tomaquag Indian Memorial Museum in Ashaway, RI. It features Eva Butler's collection of Indian artifacts.
1959	Red Wing's second husband, Daniel Congdon, dies.
1960	Princess Red Wing gives the blessing at the International Congress of Distinguished Men and Women of the World in Amsterdam.
1969	Eva Lutz Butler dies. Red Wing continues running their Tomaquag Museum.
1972	June 11, The Tomaquag Indian Memorial Museum reopens in its new home near the Dovecrest Restaurant and Indian Trading Post in Exeter, RI.
1975	Princess Red Wing is awarded Doctorate of Human Affairs from the University of Rhode Island.
1978	She is inducted into the Rhode Island Hall of Fame as Woman of the Year. Governor Joseph Garrahy declares June 23, 1978 as Princess Red Wing Day.
1982	Princess Red Wing serves on the committee that drafts "Declaration of World Thanksgiving" for the United Nations.
1987	December 2, Princess Red Wing dies at age 92.

Learn More About Princess Red Wing and the Narragansett and Wampanoag Tribes

- DeKeyser, Stacy. ***The Wampanoag.*** Franklin Watts, 2005.
- Dell, Pamela. ***The Wampanoag.*** Marshall Cavendish Benchmark, 2009.
- Ryan, Marla Felkins and Linda Schmittroth, ed. ***Narragansetts.*** Blackbirch Press, 2003.

Web site:

- Tomaquag Indian Memorial Museum: http://www.tomaquagmuseum.com/

Glossary

artifact (AR tuh fakt) An object from another time or culture.

culture (KUHL chur) The traditions, customs, and sometimes religious practices of a group of people.

Narragansett (NER uh GAN sit) The native people of the State of Rhode Island. These warriors came to the Rhode Island area over 30,000 years ago.

official seal (uh FISH uhl SEEL) A type of stamp with a special design that is printed on an important document to make it official.

powwow (PAU wau) A gathering of Native Americans that includes meetings, traditional foods, crafts, and dances.

succotash (SUHK uh tash) A Native American dish made of boiled corn and beans.

undersecretariat (UHN dur sek ruh TAIR ee uht) A department of a ministry or cabinet in which an under secretary is in charge.

Wampanoag (wahm puh NOH ag) Native American people of Rhode Island and parts of Massachusetts.

wampum (WAHM puhm) Beads carved from shells and strung together in special designs. Wampum could be made into belts and necklaces. It was sometimes used as a kind of money.

—16—

Janet Moreau Stone: Olympic Gold Medal Runner

by Laurie Toupin

It is summer, 1952. Fans from all over the world pack the Olympic track stadium in Helsinki, Finland. Janet perches on her starting block. She is the third runner in a four-person **relay**. Her job is to get the baton, run 100 meters, and pass it to the fourth person on the team. If they win, Janet will be the first native Rhode Islander to bring home an Olympic gold medal.

The gun goes off. The race begins. Janet focuses on the runner coming towards her. Her heart pounds. Suddenly, someone calls from the stands, "Hey Moreau! I'm one of your classmates!" Janet forces herself not to react. She knows that if she loses concentration, even for a second, all will be lost.

Her teammate is almost here. Janet sprints. Without looking, she reaches back for the baton.

Janet Teresa Moreau was born to Elizabeth and Arthur Moreau in Pawtucket, Rhode Island. She was the youngest of five children.

Janet taught herself to swim at the age of five. By seventh grade, she swam for the **Amateur Athletics Union (AAU)**. Janet won almost every race, breaking many records.

But swimming wasn't her future. On Field Day, high schools from all over Rhode Island sent their best athletes to compete in sporting events. Janet's coach asked her to run the 100 meter. Janet was shocked. "I am not a runner, I am a swimmer!" Janet told him. But she ran. And much to her surprise, she won.

After high school, Janet attended Boston University. Janet decided to become a physical education teacher. She continued to run and swim. Her track coach suggested that if she wanted to have a shot at the Olympics, she would have to choose. Janet chose track. The decision paid off.

In 1951, the first **Pan American Games** were held in Buenos Aires, Argentina. This sporting event brought together the best athletes in North, South, and Central America. Janet was a member of the United States 400-meter relay team. They won.

The following year, in the Olympic qualifying races, Janet tied for first with Catherine Hardy in the 100 meter. Janet won a spot on the women's Olympic team.

"I couldn't believe I was going," Janet says.

That summer Janet flew to Helsinki, Finland. Her heart raced as she walked into the Olympic stadium during opening ceremonies. More than 70,000 people roared as the United States team entered. "This is one of the greatest joys an athlete

TIDBITS

Three of Janet's teammates at the Pan American Games were African American. When the team arrived at the place where they were supposed to stay, the security guard said Janet could enter, but her teammates could not. Janet's coach said, "Okay, we're leaving." Eventually, Janet's teammates were allowed to stay. However, they were separated from their white teammates and were not allowed to eat or sleep with them.

can have," she said. "I was so proud to be there representing the United States."

At 24, Janet was the oldest member of the team. She also was the most experienced. As the second runner handed her the baton, Janet thought of nothing but running. She ran those 100 meters. She handed the baton to Catherine Hardy. Catherine crossed the finish line. The United States won the gold and set a world record.

Janet returned to Rhode Island. She was honored with a **ticker tape parade** and given a trophy.

As a child, Janet wanted to be a priest. After she retired from 36 years as a physical education teacher, Janet became a Certified Catholic Chaplain.

At the 2008 Olympics in Beijing, Janet served as an interfaith chaplain to the United States team. She helped the athletes prepare spiritually and mentally. "God has given me so much, I wanted to give something back," Janet said.

Janet Moreau and the 1952 Olympic gold medal relay team members.

TIDBITS

When Janet was young, it wasn't common for girls to be athletes. "My mom just didn't understand," says Janet. "I would come home late from practice, exhausted. I would have to eat a cold dinner, because everyone else had eaten. Mom would just ask me why I was doing this," Janet recalls. "But my dad understood. He was behind me."

Janet loves animals and horses. She raised an Arabian horse named Little Nel.

Timeline: Janet Moreau Stone

1927 ➤ October 26, Janet is born to Elizabeth and Arthur Moreau in Pawtucket, Rhode Island.

1947 ➤ Janet becomes the National Jr. 100 meter freestyle champion.

1947–1957 ➤ Janet becomes the first female to pass the rigorous surf test at Second Beach and the first female state lifeguard and water safety instructor at Sand Hill Cove.

1948 ➤ Janet wins the New England AAU 100 yard. She is chosen for the first Rhode Island All State Swimming Team.

Fall, Janet starts college at Boston University.

1949 ➤ Janet is again chosen for the Rhode Island All State Swim Team.

1949 –1952 ➤ Janet is an All American track team member. She sets a new Standing Long Jump record: 8 feet, 10 inches. The record still stands.

1950 ➤ Janet sets new records for the 100 meter run in the Jr. National Championship games.

1951 ➤ Janet runs in the first Pan American Games. She wins the gold medal in the 400 meter relay. She graduates from BU with a degree in education.

1952 ➤ Janet is the 100 meter national championship. The win qualifies her to compete in the XV Olympics. She wins the gold medal in the 4x100 meter relay.

She is chosen as athlete of the year by the Disabled American Veterans.

1955 ➤ Janet marries Ray Stone and moves to Barrington, Rhode Island. She becomes the Physical Education Instructor at the Barrington Jr. High School.

1959 ➤ Janet serves as a game official for Track and Field for the Pan American Games in Chicago, IL.

1968 ➤ The Rhode Island Heritage Hall of Fame inducts Janet as a member.

1979 ➤ Janet is inducted into the Boston University Hall of Fame.

1986 ➤ She becomes a charter member of the Pawtucket Hall of Fame.

1987 ➤ Janet is inducted into the Rhode Island Aquatic Hall of Fame.

2008 ➤ Janet serves as the interfaith chaplain for the Beijing Olympics.

Learn More About Janet Moreau Stone and the Olympics

- Boyce, Natalie Pope. and Mary Pope Osborne. ***Ancient Greece and the Olympics: A Nonfiction Companion to Hour of the Olympics (Magic Tree House Research Guide #10)***. Random House, 2004.
- Harper, Jo. ***Wilma Rudolph: Olympic Runner (Childhood of Famous Americans).*** Alladin Paperbacks. 2004.
- Marsh, Carole. ***A Fun Book of Olympic Trivia: A to Z: Including the 2000 Summer Olympics, in Sidney, Australia (Olympic Trivia for Kids).*** Gallopade International, 2000.
- Marsh, Carole. ***A Fun Book of Olympic Trivia: A to Z: Including the 2002 Winter Olympics in Salt Lake City, Utah (Olympic Trivia for Kids).***

Web sites:

- Boston University Hall of Fame: http://www.goterriers.com/hallfame/stone-janet.html
- A short biography of Janet Moreau Stone: http://www.sports-reference.com/olympics/athletes/mo/janet-moreau- 1.html

Glossary

Amateur Athletics Union –AAU (AM uh tur ath LET ik YOON yuhn) A large, volunteer organization in the United States that promotes amateur sports and physical fitness.

Pan American Games Athletic games held every four years. They are always held the summer before the Olympics.

relay (REE lay) A team race. Four runners take turns completing a part of the race. Each person carries a baton during his part of the race then passes the baton to the next runner.

ticker tape parade (TIK ur TAYP puh RADE) Ticker tapes were used in the early 1900s. They were long paper strips that were printed by machine and gave the reader the latest stock prices. These strips of paper were flung out of office windows and made a parade look like it was traveling through snow. Today, people use shredded papers instead. A ticker tape parade is a great honor.

—17—

Jacqueline Kennedy Onassis: First Lady of the United States

by Tammy Gagne

Jackie Kennedy sat proudly beside her husband as they rode through sunny downtown Dallas. The crowd cheered as the president and first lady smiled and waved. The Kennedys knew that Texas was going to be an important state in the president's upcoming re-election campaign. What they didn't know was that this trip would end one life and change countless others.

....

Jacqueline Lee Bouvier was born July 28, 1929 in Southampton, New York. Her father, Jack, worked for the New York Stock Exchange. Her mother, Janet, loved horses. Jackie also was an **equestrian**. She was a national riding champion by the time she was eleven.

Around this time Jackie's parents divorced. Her mother remarried. Jackie and her younger sister Caroline moved with their mother and new stepfather to Rhode Island.

Jackie loved reading. As she got older, she began writing poems and stories of her own. Sometimes her work was published in newspapers.

TIDBITS

In 1951 Jackie entered a contest held by *Vogue* magazine. The winner had to create an original issue of the publication including articles, illustrations, and even advertising. The prize was a year as a junior editor of the magazine. Half of this time would be spent in Paris. Jackie came in first out of 1,280 entrants. She turned down the prize because her mother didn't want her to leave the country.

After high school Jackie attended Vassar College in New York. Her junior year brought her to France as an exchange student. Jackie finished college at George Washington University.

After graduating Jackie worked for the *Washington Times-Herald*. She was the newspaper's Inquiring Camera Girl. Each day she roamed the city, photographing people and asking them a question. She would then write an article about their responses. Many of her questions were about **politics**.

She met some famous people during this time. Her first interview was with Pat Nixon, wife of Vice President Richard Nixon. She met Massachusetts congressman John F. Kennedy. Jackie didn't know it yet, but he was the man she would later marry.

The American people adored the Kennedy family. Jackie's wedding to John drew national attention. Many people saw the pair as the perfect couple. Both husband and wife were young, smart, and full of **ambition**.

The couple's first child was born in 1957. They named her Caroline after Jackie's sister.

In 1960 John ran for president. At first Jackie joined him on the campaign trail. Soon she became pregnant again. Jackie's doctor told her to stay home until the baby was born. She didn't stop helping, though. She answered letters, recorded commercials, and gave interviews. She wrote a newspaper column called *Campaign Wife*.

That November, John won the election. A little over two

weeks later, Jackie delivered John F. Kennedy, Jr. The young family's story seemed like it was straight out of a story book. Later, people called the Kennedy presidency *Camelot*. This was the name of a popular musical about the legend of King Arthur.

The fairy tale took a tragic turn on November 22, 1963. During a visit to Texas, President Kennedy was shot and killed. A man named Lee Harvey Oswald was arrested for the **assassination**.

Jackie moved her family to New York. She helped to create the John F. Kennedy Presidential Library and Museum in Boston, Massachusetts.

Jackie remarried in 1968. Her second husband was a businessman named Aristotle Onassis. She was widowed again in 1975.

The next phase of Jackie's life brought her back to something she loved dearly: books. She accepted a job as an **editor** for Viking Press in New York City. She later worked for Doubleday as a senior editor.

Jacqueline Bouvier Kennedy Onassis died in New York on May 19, 2004. She was buried in Arlington National Cemetery beside her first husband, President John F. Kennedy.

One of Jackie's first jobs was the Inquiring Camera Girl for the Washington-Times Herald *newspaper.*

TIDBITS

After the Kennedys married, John had two back operations. Jackie urged him to spend his recovery time writing. His book, *Profiles in Courage*, won a Pulitzer Prize in 1957.

Jackie once said, "If you bungle raising your children, I don't think whatever else you do matters very much."

Jackie was known for her sense of style. She is still considered an American fashion icon.

Timeline: Jacqueline Kennedy Onassis

1929 ➢	July 28, Jacqueline Lee Bouvier is born in Southampton, New York to Jack and Janet Bouvier.
1933 ➢	March 3, Jackie's sister, Caroline Lee Bouvier, is born.
1951 ➢	Jackie graduates from George Washington University and begins working for the *Washington Times-Herald*.
1952 ➢	John is elected to the U.S. Senate.
1953 ➢	September 12, Jackie marries John Fitzgerald Kennedy in Newport, Rhode Island.
1957 ➢	November 27, the Kennedy's first child, Caroline Bouvier Kennedy, is born.
1960 ➢	November 8, John is elected President of the United States.
	November 25, John and Jackie's second child, John F. Kennedy, Jr., is born.
1963 ➢	August 7, John and Jackie's third child, Patrick Bouvier Kennedy, is born. He dies two days later.
	November 22, President Kennedy is assassinated.
1968 ➢	October 20, Jackie marries Aristotle Onassis, a business man from Greece.
1975 ➢	March 15, Aristotle Onassis dies.
	Jackie accepts a position as editor for Viking Press in New York City.
1994 ➢	May 19, Jacqueline Kennedy Onassis dies in New York City.

Learn More About Jacqueline Kennedy Onassis

- Raatma, Lucia Tarbox. ***Jacqueline Kennedy***. Capstone Press, 2010.

Web sites:

- John F. Kennedy Presidential Library and Museum: http://www.jfklibrary.org/JFK/Life-of-Jacqueline-B-Kennedy.aspx
- National First Ladies' Library: http://www.firstladies.org/biographies/firstladies.aspx?biography=36

Glossary

ambition (am BISH uhn) Having a strong wish and drive to be successful.

assassination (uh SASS uh NAY shuhn) The murder of an important or well-known person such as a king, president, etc.

editor (ED uh tur) Someone who checks the contents of a book, newspaper, or magazine and gets it ready to be published.

equestrian (i KWESS tree uhn) A person who rides and trains horses.

politics (POL uh tiks) The activities of politicians and political parties regarding the running of a government.

—18—

Ruth Buzzi: Actor and Comedian

by Laurie Toupin

Ruth Buzzi felt nervous. She was next to audition for the musical "Sweet Charity." She forced herself to concentrate on the part. When she finished, everyone in the room was laughing. This was good since it was suppose to be a comedy. But then the director, Bob Fosse, asked her to sing "Blue Moon." She knew the tune but didn't know the words. So she sang about giraffes, pirates, sailboats.

Bob waved his hands telling her to stop. "We'll be in touch with your agent," he said.

Ruth Ann Buzzi was born July 24, 1936 to Rena and Angelo Buzzi in Westerly, Rhode Island.

Ruth had a knack for making people laugh. When she was 10, her ballet teacher asked her to do a special comedy piece for the annual **recital**. The audience loved Ruth's number. For the first time, Ruth felt the power of making people laugh.

When Ruth graduated from high school, her dad encouraged her to fly to California to study acting. She was the first in her family to set foot on an airplane. "Dad believed in me 100% from the beginning...," says Ruth.

After graduating from the Pasadena Playhouse, she moved to New York. She started doing commercials and off-Broadway parts almost immediately. She performed comedy routines in night clubs.

Then Bob Fosse, the director of *Sweet Charity*, called. He said he wanted her for several parts in the play, including a singing fairy. Ruth thought her wildest dreams had come true.

But her real break into acting was yet to come.

A new comedy **variety show** was being **piloted**, *Rowan and Martin's Laugh-In*. A friend suggested Ruth try out. She didn't want to leave Broadway, but auditioned anyway. Dan Rowan and Dick Martin loved her.

Laugh-In made television history. It poked fun of everything and everyone including political figures. It was fast paced. Everybody wanted to be on it, even Vice-president Richard Nixon. The show became the most popular TV comedy of its time. Ruth became one of its most popular stars. She also was one of only four characters to appear on every episode of the show.

Often comedians make up their own characters. Ruth created several. But none were as famous as Gladys Ormphby. Gladys was a **spinster**, an older woman who never married. She was always seeking romance. She wore an oversized brown sweater, hair net, and saggy brown stockings. She carried a purse that doubled as a weapon. If any one said

TIDBITS

Ruth was head cheerleader in high school. She used comedy to fire up the student body before football games.

While at the Pasadena Playhouse, Ruth studied voice, dance, and acting. She also took courses in **cosmetology** in case her acting career didn't take off.

Ruth performed as Gladys outside of *Laugh-In*. Gladys appeared on a number of TV shows over the next 30 years.

anything Gladys thought was not proper towards a lady, she hit them hard!

Ruth could play everything from a singing southern bell to a character like Gladys. For this unique ability, she won a Golden Globe for Best Supporting Actress on *Laugh-In.*

During the 1990s, Ruth appeared on *Sesame Street* where she played "Ruthie," the owner of Finders Keepers. She loved working in children's television. She was nominated for an **Emmy award** five years in a row for these performances.

Ruth also worked for Disney on a number of films. She did voiceovers for Mama on the *Bernstein Bears*, and played in *Freaky Friday* and *The Apple Dumpling Gang Rides Again*. So far, Ruth has done more than 20 movies and made more than 200 TV appearances.

Today, Ruth lives on a ranch in Texas with her husband.

Ruth Buzzi as Gladys Ormphby with comedian Flip Wilson on Laugh-in.

TIDBITS

When Ruth first arrived in New York, she teamed up with another start-up comedian, Dom DeLuise. Dom played a magician. Ruth played Shakuntula, his always grinning assistant who never said a word. The two became wildly popular. They performed in night clubs and even appeared on a television.

Ruth won the much desired **CLIO award** for Best Spokesperson in a television commercial for her series of Clorox-2 commercials.

Timeline: Ruth Buzzi

1936 ➤ July 24, Ruth Buzzi is born to Rena and Angelo Buzzi.

1953 ➤ Ruth flies to California to study at the Pasadena Playhouse.

1959 ➤ Ruth comes to New York. She creates the character Shakuntula, a grinning magician's assistant who says nothing.

1961 ➤ Ruth performs in *Auntie Mame*, an off-Broadway production.

1965 ➤ Ruth joins the cast of a CBS TV show called *The Entertainers*.

1966 ➤ She joins the cast of Broadway's *Sweet Charity*.

1967 ➤ Ruth appears on the *Steve Allen Comedy Hour*.

1968 ➤ Ruth begins a six-year job on a new comedy variety series, *Rowan and Martin's Laugh-In.*

1971 ➤ Ruth is inducted into the Rhode Island Heritage Hall of Fame.

1973 ➤ She wins the Golden Globe award for Best Supporting Actress on the *Rowan and Martin's Laugh-In* show.

1975 ➤ Ruth stars in the kid show *Far Out Space Nuts.*

1977 ➤ Disney Productions asks Ruth to perform in *Freaky Friday.*

1978 ➤ December 10, Ruth marries her current husband, Kent Perkins.

1979 ➤ Ruth plays in the Disney movie *The Apple Dumpling Gang Rides Again.*

1993 to 1999 ➤ Ruth plays "Ruthie" on Sesame Street. As a result of her work, she was nominated for five Emmy Awards.

2002 ➤ Ruth is inducted into the Television Hall of Fame.

2008 ➤ The Board of Regents of Northwood University named Ruth a "Distinguished Woman of Northwood."

Learn More About Ruth Buzzi and Women in Comedy

- Schuman, Michael A. ***Tina Fey: TV Comedy Superstar (People to Know Today)***. Enslow, 2011.
- Sharp, Katie. ***Ellen Degeneres (People in the News)***. Lucent Books, 2010.
- Stewart, Gail. ***History Makers - Great Women Comedians***. Lucent Books, 2002.

Web sites:

- A short biography of Ruth Buzzi: http://www.fandango.com/ruthbuzzi/biography/p9987
- An interview with Ruth Buzzi: http://www.ycdtotv.com/wtyo/index.php?p=buzzi_interview

Glossary

CLIO Award Trophies given each year for the best advertisements. The award is named for the Greek goddess Clio.

cosmetology (koz muh TAWL uh jee) The study of hair and skin care and the products used for such care.

Emmy Award Trophies given each year for the best programs on television.

piloted (PYE luht uhd) In this story, tried out, started, done as an experiment.

recital (ri SYE tuhl) A performance done by a single person or small group; often a musical performance done by students.

spinster (SPIN sutr) An older woman who has never been married.

variety show (vuh RYE uh tee SHOH) A television program that featured music, dance, and comedy skits.

— 19 —

Jennifer Murray: Record-Breaking Helicopter Pilot

by Cheryl Mansfield

Jennifer glanced at her co-pilot. She saw the fear on his face. She felt the same fear. They should have landed hours ago. They should have paid more attention to the weather. Now snow blinded them. Her heart raced. She hung on tight. The helicopter shook. They were going to crash.

. . . .

Jennifer Murray was born in Providence, Rhode Island. Her father was Sir William Mather, a British business man. Her mother was Lady Eleanor Mather. When Jennifer was very young her family returned to England.

From an early age Jennifer liked adventure. She liked to travel to foreign countries. She hiked through **Nepal** and **Bhutan**. She liked to run marathons.

Jennifer also had an artistic side. She went to the Central School of Arts and Crafts in London. She majored in Textile Design. Shortly after graduation Jennifer married Simon Murray. They moved to Thailand.

Jennifer opened a textile business. She sold fabric from around the world.

In 1994, Simon bought a half share in a helicopter. He didn't have time to fly. He suggested Jennifer take lessons. Jennifer loved flying. She decided to get her pilot's license. Simon eventually got his license, too. Together they flew on longer and longer trips. Jennifer began to wonder what it would be like to fly around the world.

Three years later Jennifer's daydream turned into reality. She teamed with pilot Colin Bodill to fly around the world from east to west. The trip earned her a spot in the ***Guinness Book of World Records***. But Jennifer wasn't satisfied. She wanted to fly the trip solo.

In 2000, Jennifer tried again. This time Colin flew in a separate helicopter. The trip was a success earning Jennifer another spot in the *Guinness Book of World Records*. But it wasn't enough. Jennifer wanted to fly around the world from the North Pole to the South Pole.

In 2003, she and Colin set out on the journey. But they ran into trouble. Two days after passing the South Pole they hit bad weather in **Antarctica.** Their helicopter crashed in a blizzard. The temperature was minus 50 degrees. Jennifer suffered several broken bones. It took rescuers four and a half hours to find them.

Many people thought Jennifer would stop flying. But she said, "There's some unfinished business when you attempt a record like this and fail. The only way to lay that to rest is to

TIDBITS

The trip around the world from North Pole to South Pole took 171 days to complete. They traveled 32,206 **nautical** miles. They made 126 stops for fuel in 30 countries.

In remote areas of the world, fuel was stored in advance. They found it by using a **Global Positioning System.** The most dangerous part of the trip was the 500 miles between South America and Antarctica. It was over open water.

finish the job." In December of 2006, Colin and Jennifer took off from an airport in Texas. Once again they would attempt to fly around the world from the North Pole to the South Pole. This time they watched weather conditions very closely. They landed the helicopter when they hit bad weather in Antarctica. They spent many days in tents and abandoned huts waiting for the weather to clear. In May of 2007 they touched down in Texas. They had flown around the world. They had finished the job.

Today Jennifer talks to groups about her story. She tells of desert heat, freezing Polar Regions and dangerous oceans. When she is asked what she likes best about flying, she replies, "You are a bird, you can soar, you have the freedom of the sky. . ."

Jennifer's helicopter can be seen at the Smithsonian's Air & Space Museum.

TIDBITS

The helicopter Jennifer flew on both her trips around the world is now in the Smithsonian Air & Space Museum in Washington, D.C.

When not flying, Jennifer likes to go to the gym, jog, and paint. She also enjoys spending time with her three children and five grandchildren.

Timeline: Jennifer Murray

1940 ➤ June, Jennifer is born in Providence, Rhode Island to British citizens Sir William and Lady Eleanor Mather.

1944 ➤ The Mather family returns to England.

1961 ➤ Jennifer graduates from the Central School of Arts & Crafts, in London. She majors in Textile Design.

1966 ➤ Jennifer works in London as a textile designer.

Jennifer marries Simon Murray and they move to Thailand. She starts a textile company.

1967 ➤ Their son, Justin, is born.

1969 ➤ Jennifer sells the textile company and the family moves to Hong Kong. Daughters Suzanna and Christy are born.

1994 ➤ At her husband's suggestion, Jennifer takes helicopter flying lessons and receives her pilot's license.

1997 ➤ Jennifer becomes the first female pilot to fly a helicopter around the world. She had a co-pilot. She enters the *Guinness Book of World Records*.

1998 ➤ She goes on a lecture tour. She prepares to fly solo around the world.

2000 ➤ Jennifer is the first woman to fly solo around the world in a helicopter. She also is the first person to fly around the world without auto pilot.

Jennifer comes in third in the London-to-Sydney Air Race. She sets a world record as the fastest female pilot to fly around the world.

2003 ➤ Jennifer and co-pilot, Colin Bodill become the first pilots to fly a single engine helicopter across the **Drake Passage**.

Jennifer and Colin attempt to fly Pole to Pole. They crash in Antarctica.

2004 ➤ **The Republic of The Gambia** issues a postage stamp in Jennifer's honor.

2005 ➤ Jennifer is inducted into the Rhode Island Aviation Hall of Fame.

2006 ➤ December 6th, Jennifer and her co-pilot Colin Bodill leave Texas on a second attempt to fly around the world – Pole to Pole.

2007 ➤ May, they complete their trip. Jennifer becomes the first female to fly around the world, both around the Earth's **circumference** and from North Pole to South Pole.

Learn More About Jennifer Murray, Helicopters, and Explorers

- Boyer Binns, Tristan. ***Exploring Antarctica.*** Heinemann, 2007.
- Stille, Darlene Ruth. ***Helicopters.*** Compass Point Books, 2004.
- Reed, Jennifer. ***Daring American Heroes of Flight, Nine Brave Fliers.*** Enslow Publishers, Inc., 2009.

Web sites:

- See pictures and read diary entries about Jennifer's North to South Pole flight: www.PolarFirst.com

Glossary

Antarctica (ant ARK ti kuh) The continent that surrounds the South Pole.

Bhutan (BOO tahn) A country in Asia found on the northeast border of India.

circumference (sur KUHM fur uhnss) The outer edge of a circle.

Drake Passage (DRAYK PASS ij) The body of water located between the tip of South America and the South Shetland Islands of Antarctica. It is known to have some of the roughest seas on earth.

Global Positioning System (GLOH buhl puh ZISH uhn ing SISS tuhm) Also called a GPS. A type of computer that gives a person his accurate position on earth by getting information from at least four satellites. A GPS can also give accurate time and weather information.

Guinness Book of World Records (GIN ess BUK of WURLD REK urdz) A list that is collected annually of important records completed by people (such as the tallest man or the largest collection of radios) or by nature (such as the hottest temperature reached on earth).

nautical (NAW tuh kuhl) In this story, a way to measure distance on the sea or in the air. A nautical mile equals 6,076 feet.

Nepal (nuh PAWL) A small Asian country located between India and China.

Republic of The Gambia (ri PUHB lik of the GAM bee uh) The smallest country in West Africa. It is bounded by Senegal and has a small coastline on the Atlantic Ocean.

—20—

Joyce Jillson: Actress, Author, Astrologer

by Barbara Keevil Parker

People in Hollywood called Joyce Jillson the "Hollywood **Astrologer.**" Joyce gave astrological advice to movie stars, politicians, and athletes.

One day, Twentieth Century Fox movie studio called. The person calling wanted her help. Would she **predict** "lucky" opening dates for a Twentieth Century Fox film?

Joyce was delighted. She asked the name of the movie they wanted her to predict.

The studio would call the movie *Star Wars.*

Joyce needed to consult her charts. By consulting stars in the universe, she predicted events and successes before they happened.

When she called back, she told them to open *Star Wars* on May 25, 1977.

The studio released the film on that date. The movie became a huge success.

Joyce Jillson was born December 26, 1945 in Cranston, Rhode Island.

When Joyce was eight years old, she became fascinated with the stars. She studied astrology with Maude Williams, an astrologer. Williams predicted Joyce would have a career in astrology. By age 10, Joyce was making predictions on adult topics like the stock market and politics.

After high school, she studied at the New England Conservatory of Music in Boston. For two years, she sang in Boston nightclubs. She won a scholarship to study opera at Boston University.

From Boston, Joyce traveled to New York City. She starred in the Broadway play, "La Grosse Valise" in New York and Paris. She was the **lead** in "The Roar of the Greasepaint - the Smell of the Crowd." Her beautiful singing voice was featured on the original cast album. She won an acting award as the outstanding Broadway newcomer.

Joyce moved to Los Angeles. She acted on the television program, "Peyton Place." She played the role of Jill for 120 **episodes**. She performed in films and on television.

Through her life, Joyce used astrology to guide her career. In 1973, Joyce began presenting **horoscope** reports on Los Angeles radio and television. On her television show, "The Joyce Jillson Show," she discussed astrology and interviewed celebrities.

In 1988, Donald Regan, a former white house chief-of-staff, said First Lady Nancy Reagan often spoke with an astrologer.

Reporters asked Joyce if she had advised the President.

TIDBITS

Some people believe astrology is a dependable way to predict the future. Astrologists think the position of the sun, moon and planets at the time of birth, affects our minds, emotions, bodies and careers. Many people enjoy reading their horoscopes in the newspaper to see what they predict about their lives. Jillson believed astrology could help pinpoint people's talents, their good times and bad times. Other people feel astrology is a false science.

TIDBITS

Businesses asked Joyce for advice. Twentieth Century Fox Studio asked her to predict the best days for new movies to open in theaters. She helped Ford Motor Company choose the date to introduce a new car, the Taurus. She was the official astrologer for the Los Angeles Dodgers for two years. Joyce made charts for company executives of their colleagues and competitors. Movie directors asked which cast would bring home an Oscar.

Joyce claimed Reagan aides paid her $1200 in 1980 for advice on possible running mates for Ronald Reagan. Joyce recommended Mr. Reagan choose George H.W. Bush as his vice-presidential running mate. They won the election.

Newspaper headlines called her "The Astrologer Who Runs the White House." She was famous overnight. She became a guest on television shows. Articles about her appeared in magazines and newspapers.

The Reagans denied knowing Joyce Jillson. Whether she gave advice to the Reagans remains unclear. She claimed she did.

Joyce wrote ten astrology books and two popular books. *Real Women Don't Pump Gas* was a New York Times bestselling book. Her columns appeared in 230 United States newspapers and 84 newspapers around the world.

Joyce founded and funded the Women's Equalization Committee. Its goal was to help women find equality at home and at work. As a result, CBS featured her in a "60 Minutes" report.

Joyce loved raising Great Dane dogs, playing chess, and traveling. Two books, *Joyce Jillson's Astrology for Dogs* and *Joyce Jillson's Astrology for Cats,* were published after her death.

Joyce Jillson died October 1, 2004 of kidney failure. She was 58.

The cover of one of Joyce's books.

Timeline: Joyce Jillson

1945 ➤ December 26, Joyce Jillson is born in Cranston, Rhode Island.

1949 ➤ Her parents end their marriage.

1953 ➤ At age 8, she finds astrology interesting.

1955 ➤ Joyce starts giving astrology readings at age 10.

1959–62 ➤ Joyce attends Cranston High School West. She leaves after her junior year. Later she finishes school in a home-school program.

1964 ➤ She gets a small role in an episode of "The Man from U.N.C.L.E."

1965 ➤ She appears on Broadway in "The Roar of the Greasepaint—The Smell of the Crowd." She wins a theatre award as outstanding newcomer.

1968 ➤ Joyce wins a big role in the soap opera, *Peyton Place*. She plays the character, Jill, in 120 episodes.

1969 ➤ She and Joseph Gallagher marry. They divorce in 1981.

1973 ➤ She plays the title role in the movie, *Superchicks.*

She starts presenting horoscope reports on Los Angeles television.

She begins "The Joyce Jillson Show" from Los Angeles.

1977 ➤ On her advice, Twentieth Century Fox opens the movie, *Star Wars,* on May 25.

1980 ➤ Joyce claims to help President Ronald Reagan choose George H.W. Bush as his running mate.

1981 ➤ The people of Cranston, Rhode Island, induct her into the Cranston Hall of Fame.

1994 ➤ Joyce hires Holiday Mathis as an assistant. She calls her "Astro Girl."

2004 ➤ October 1, Joyce Jillson dies at Cedars Sinai Medical Center in Los Angeles. She has kidney failure. She is 58.

Learn More About Joyce Jillson and Astrology

- Asselin, Kristine Carlson. ***Taurus, Virgo, and Capricorn: All about the EARTH Signs.*** Capstone Press, 2010.
- Crawford, Gregory. ***Animals in the Stars: Chinese Astrology for Children***. Bear Cub Books, 2002.
- Jones, Jen. ***Gemini, Libra, and Aquarius: All about the AIR Signs.*** Capstone Press, 2010.
- Marks, Jennifer L. ***Aries, Leo, and Sagittarius: All about the FIRE signs.*** Capstone Press, 2010.

Web sites:

- A biography of Joyce Jillson: http://wp.jeremysilman.com/astrology/jillson_bio.html
- Read a short tribute to Joyce Jillson: http://www.solsticepoint.com/astrologersmemorial/jillson.html

Glossary

astrologer (uh STROL uh jer) A person who believes that the positions of the stars and planets can influence people's lives and futures.

episodes (EP uh sohdz) Individual programs in a TV series.

horoscope (HOR uh skope) A chart based on the positions of the stars and planets on the day someone was born. Astrologers believe they can predict events in a person's life by using this type of chart.

lead (LEED) In this story, the main actor in show, movie, or play.

predict (pri DIKT) To tell what will happen in the future.

—21—

Claudine Schneider:

Congresswoman and Environmental Leader

by Linda Crotta Brennan

The doctor told Claudine that she had cancer. She had a fifty/fifty chance of surviving. She was only twenty-five.

Claudine prayed that she might live. She said, "How can I possibly die without fulfilling my purpose?"

....

Claudine was born in Pennsylvania on March 25, 1947. Claudine's father, Ted Cmarada, ran a men's clothing store. Her mother, Nenette, was from Belgium. They taught her that each person is on earth for a purpose. They said, "You can be anything you set your mind to."

In college, Claudine majored in languages. She studied in Spain. Claudine wanted to be a peacemaker and see the world. So she applied to be a **diplomat**. While waiting to hear, she took a job in Washington, D.C. It was with an environmental education organization. There, she met and fell in love with Dr. Eric Schneider. The couple married and moved to Rhode Island.

Soon after, Claudine discovered she had cancer. She focused on finding her purpose, her reason to live. She wanted to leave the planet a better place. Claudine organized the community. Her group fought the construction of a nuclear power plant in Rhode Island. The plant was never built. Then Claudine founded the Conservation Law Foundation. It used law to protect the environment. She was made the coordinator managing Rhode Island's coast.

The Republican Party asked Claudine's husband to run for governor. He said no. Then the party asked Claudine to run for the U.S. **House of Representatives**. She agreed. Her opponent was Edward Beard. He was the **incumbent**, which means he already held the office. Claudine lost, but not by much.

She became a television producer and hosted a talk show, putting her in the public eye. When she ran against Beard again in 1980, she won. Claudine was the first woman ever to represent Rhode Island in the U.S. Congress. She was well-liked and was reelected to four more **terms.**

Claudine agreed with the Republican Party about finances. She was careful to balance the budget. She worked to cut **inflation**.

Claudine was also interested in the environment, women's health, justice, and peace. She didn't always agree with her party. She often voted against Republican President Reagan's policies. President Reagan wanted to build a nuclear power plant in Tennessee. Claudine argued against it. The project was stopped.

In 1990, Claudine decided to leave the House of

TIDBITS

Odds were against Claudine when she first ran for office. She was woman. She was young. She had no experience in government. She didn't have a lot of money. And she was a Republican in a very Democratic state.

Claudine worked with fellow representative George Brown to create a television program called *Congress Bridge*. It featured a series of discussions between the legislature of the Soviet Union and the U.S. Congress.

Representatives. Instead she ran for the **Senate** against Claiborne Pell. Pell was in his seventies. But he was still very popular. Claudine lost the election.

Claudine left politics, but not public service. She helped run a world-wide renewable energy company. She convinced fifty major companies to reduce their greenhouse gasses.

She served on President Clinton's Competitiveness Council. It looked for ways to make our country an **economic** leader. She also taught at Harvard's School of Government.

Claudine moved to Boulder, CO because of its beautiful mountains. She developed cancer again. But she fought it off. Today, she works helping businesses, governments, and schools become **sustainable.**

When asked which of her accomplishments gives her the most satisfaction, Claudine says, "The next one!" She tells people, "Respect all living and non-living things. Know that you are here on this earth to make a better world. You can do anything you set your heart and mind to doing. *Anything*!"

In 1981, Claudine Schneider helped to stop funding for the Clinch River nuclear reactor in Tennessee.

TIDBITS

One of the laws that Claudine helped to pass created Energy Star ratings. They help people buy appliances that use less electricity.

In her last year in Congress, Claudine proposed the "Global Warming Protection Act." This law would have allowed the government to save money and reduce global warming. It did not pass.

Timeline: Claudine Schneider

1947 ➤ March 25, Claudine is born to Ted and Nenette Cmarada in Clairton, PA.

1969 ➤ Claudine receives **BA** in languages from Windham College, Vermont. She moves to Washington, D.C. and takes a job with an environmental education program.

1970 ➤ Claudine marries Eric Schneider. When he gets a job as a research scientist at the University of Rhode Island, the couple moves to Narragansett, R.I.

1973 ➤ Claudine founds the R.I. Committee on Energy. She is diagnosed with Hodgkin's disease, a rare form of cancer of the lymph nodes.

1973–1977 ➤ She is the Executive Director of the Conservation Law Foundation. Her citizen's group halts construction of a nuclear power plant in R.I.

1978 ➤ Claudine runs for U.S. House of Representatives against Edward Beard and loses by a slim margin.

1978–79 ➤ She is the producer and host of the *Public Affairs* television program.

1981–1991 ➤ Claudine serves in the U.S. House of Representatives for the state of Rhode Island as a Republican.

1985 ➤ She divorces Eric Schneider.

1990 ➤ Claudine loses the race for the U.S. Senate against Senator Claiborne Pell.

1991 ➤ She co-founds Energia Global, a consulting firm that focuses on renewable energy and energy efficiency. She accepts a teaching position at the John F. Kennedy School of Government at Harvard University.

1992 ➤ President Clinton appoints Claudine to the Competitiveness Policy Council.

1994 ➤ She moves to Boulder, CO.

1999 ➤ Claudine is diagnosed with cancer for a second time.

2007 ➤ She is nominated by the EPA for its Global Climate Protection Award.

1996–Present ➤ Ms. Schneider serves as a consultant for environmental and economic programs.

Learn More About Claudine Schneider and Other Women in Congress

- Morin, Isobel V. ***Women of the United States Congress***. Oliver Press, 1994.
- Pollack, Jill. ***Women on the Hill: A History of Women in Congress.*** Franklin Watts, 1996.

Web sites:

- "Claudine Schneider," *Women in Congress:* http://history.house.gov/People/Listing/S/SCHNEIDER,-Claudine-(S000136)/
- "Claudine Schneider," Claudine Schneider web site: www.claudineschneider.com

Glossary

BA Abbreviation for **B**achelor of **A**rts Degree (BACH uh lur of ARTSS di GREE) The diploma received after 4 years of college study.

diplomat (DIP luh mat) A person who represents his country's government in a foreign country.

economic (ek uh NOM ik) Having to do with money and its use in society.

House of Representatives (HOUSS of rep ri ZEN tuh tivz) One of the two sections of the U.S. Congress that makes laws for the country. It has 435 members. States send representatives according to how many people live in the state.

incumbent (in KUHM bent) A person elected to or holding a political office.

inflation (in FLAY shuhn) An increase in the amount of money that it costs to buy goods.

Senate (SEN it) One of the two sections of the U.S. Congress that makes laws for the country. Each state sends only 2 senators to Washington, D.C.

sustainable (suh STAYN uh buhl) Using natural resources (such as oil, gas, trees, etc.) so that the resource is not used up or permanently damaged.

terms (TURMZ) In this story, certain amounts of time. For example, terms in Congress are either two years or six years long.

—22—

O. Rogeriee Thompson: A Judge for Changing Times

by Cheryl Kirk Noll

Rogeriee loved her family. She loved her community in Greenville, South Carolina. But when she had a chance to go to eleventh grade at Scarsdale, NY, she jumped at it.

In Greenville, white and black communities were **segregated**. People of different races went to separate schools, restaurants, and parks. It was the law.

New York didn't have segregation laws. But Scarsdale wasn't exactly what Rogeriee expected. It was almost as segregated as Greenville. There were only four black students in her entire high school. Had she made the right choice?

Ojetta Rogeriee Thompson was born in South Carolina in 1951. Her mother was a schoolteacher and her father was a principal.

Rogeriee went to a Catholic school through eighth grade. The nuns were white, but the students were black. She went to ninth grade at an all-black high school. She expected to go to a black college and become an educator, like her parents.

Then she went to a six-week summer camp at Knoxville College in Tennessee. At camp, she heard about the Student Transfer Education Program. Qualified students could attend a high school in Scarsdale, a rich town in New York.

"Experience as much as you can before you die," she thought.

When she arrived in Scarsdale, the change was complete **culture shock**. "I'd never been around white folks," she said. But Rogeriee worked hard. Laws that had limited black people and women were being changed. She wanted to be part of the change.

After high school, Rogeriee went to college in Providence, Rhode Island. She attended Pembroke, the women's College of Brown University. A year after she started school, Pembroke combined with the men's college.

Rogeriee saw that laws and court decisions were slowly making a difference. New opportunities were opening for both blacks and women. Schools in her hometown of Greenville had **integrated** because of a Supreme Court ruling that happened when she was a young child.

Rogeriee decided to study law. She graduated from Boston University Law School in 1976.

Her first job was with Rhode Island Legal Services. Later, she opened her own law firm. She learned about Native American law when she worked for the Narragansett Indian Tribe. She was also worked as a lawyer for the City of Providence. She married William C. Clifton, and they had three children.

TIDBITS

Rogeriee lived away from home during eleventh grade. When she returned to SC wearing an **Afro**, her mother didn't approve. Rogeriee reminded her that it was 1968. Then Rogeriee went to church wearing another new style, a pantsuit. As she remembers, "Momma... just lost it. She made a scene in church and everything, and the minister even had to come to the house to console her: 'Now Sister Sarah, times are changing...'"

TIDBITS

The United States Court of Appeals is a federal court that hears appeals from District courts located within its circuit. The First Circuit has six full-time judges. It is based in Boston. It includes Maine, Massachusetts, New Hampshire, Puerto Rico and Rhode Island.

Judge Thompson tells students to learn "one step at a time. But don't be afraid to take chances, to try things. Don't be afraid of failure."

In 1988, the governor of Rhode Island appointed Ms. Thompson to the Rhode Island **District Court**. After serving for nine years, she was appointed associate justice of the Rhode Island **State Superior Court**. She was the first black woman to serve on these courts.

Judge Thompson worked to get **interpreters** for people who didn't speak English. She tried to settle up to twenty-five cases a day.

Outside of court, Judge Thompson was involved with her community. She served on the **board of trustees** for many organizations.

In 2009, both of Rhode Island's Senators recommended Judge Thompson for a seat on the Federal **Appeals** Court. President Barack Obama nominated her.

A Senate committee asked her what the role of a judge was. Her reply: justice for all and to apply the law to the facts. Her rulings, she said, are based "solely on the law."

In 2010, the United States Senate approved her **unanimously**, 98-0. Judge Thompson became the first black woman to serve as a full judge on the U.S. Federal Court of Appeals for the 1st Circuit.

Judge Thompson was inducted into the Reverend Martin Luther King Jr. Hall of Fame in 2010 by Providence Mayor David Cicilline.

Timeline: O. Rogeriee Thompson

- **1951** ➤ August 8, Ojetta Rogeriee Thompson is born in Anderson, SC.
- **1967** ➤ Rogeriee begins her junior year at Scarsdale High School through the Scarsdale Student Transfer Education Program (STEP).
- **1969** ➤ Rogeriee graduates from Scarsdale High School.
- **1973** ➤ Ojetta Rogeriee Thompson graduates from Pembroke/Brown University.
- **1974** ➤ Ms. Thompson works as a legal intern at RI Legal Services, Inc.
- **1976** ➤ Ms. Thompson graduates from Boston University Law School.
- **1976–79** ➤ She practices law as a staff attorney at RI Legal Services as a Reginald Heber Smith Fellow.
- **1979–1980** ➤ Ms. Thompson works as an associate for McKinnon and Fortunato.
- **1980–1984** ➤ O. Rogeriee Thompson has her own law firm.
- **1980–1982** ➤ Ms. Thompson is Assistant City Solicitor for Providence, RI.
- **1984–1988** ➤ She is senior partner in the law firm of Thompson & Thompson, Attorneys at Law, with her sister.
- **1988-1997** ➤ O. Rogeriee Thompson is appointed to sit on the RI District Court by Governor Edward DiPrete.
- **1997** ➤ Governor Lincoln Almond appoints Judge Thompson to Associate Justice of the RI Superior Court.
- **2010** ➤ The U.S. Senate votes unanimously to approve Rhode Island Superior Court Judge O. Rogeriee Thompson on the Boston-based Federal Court of Appeals for the first Circuit.

Learn More About Judge Ojetta Rogeriee Thompson, Her Times, and the Courts

- Shelton, Paula Young and Raul Colon. ***Child of the Civil Rights Movement.*** Schwartz & Wade, 2009.
- Gorman, Jacqueline Laks. ***Judge (Know Your Government)***. Weekly Reader Early Learning Library, 2009.

Web sites:

- More about Judge Thompson:
  http://tinyurl.com/csxrt33
  http://tinyurl.com/y8wgupx

Glossary

Afro (AF roh) A hair style made popular in the 1970's by the African American community. It featured natural curls in a full, round style.

appeals (uh PEELZ) A part of the court system in which cases are heard again, often with new or additional evidence, with the hope that the original court's decision can be changed.

board of trustees (BORD uhv truhss TEEZ) A group of people who run an organization or business.

culture shock (KUHL chur SHOK) Difficulty adjusting to a way of life that is different than your own.

district court (DISS trikt KORT) A court of law that hears trials in an area established by the federal government.

integrated (IN tuh gray tuhd) Included people of all races.

interpreters (in TUR prit urs) People who translate one language to another.

segregated (SEG ruh GAY tuhd) Kept people or things apart from the main group.

state superior court (STATE suh PIHR ee ur KORT) A state trial court with the power to hear and decide civil or criminal action which is not heard in some other court.

unanimously (you NAN uh muhss lee) Agreed on by everyone.

—23—

Martha McSally

Warrior Pilot

by Tabatha Yeatts

Martha liked the Air Force Academy. She was determined to do well there. There were some difficulties, though. Martha was too short to become a pilot. The military also had a rule that said women couldn't be fighter pilots. Martha told her teacher that she planned to fly into combat. Her teacher laughed. Martha would see about that!

Martha McSally was born in Warwick, Rhode Island in 1966. Martha was the youngest of Bernard and Eleanor McSally's five children. Bernard died of a heart attack when Martha was twelve. "It rocked my world," she said. Before her father died, Martha promised to make him proud. She has worked her whole life to live up to that promise.

In 1984, Martha entered the U.S. Air Force Academy in Colorado. As a child, she had never considered being a pilot. She tended to get motion sickness. She was short. But once Martha decided she did want to fly, she didn't let anything stop her. She convinced the academy leader to give her physical tests. She proved her height was not a problem.

Martha wanted to be a fighter pilot. That wasn't a choice for her, though. The U.S. government had a rule that women could not go into combat. After she graduated from the Air Force Academy, Martha kept studying. She attended Harvard University. At Harvard, she studied **public policy**.

In 1991, Congress voted to change the combat rule. Women *could* be fighter pilots. But the military still needed to change its rule against it. Two years later, they did. Martha was chosen as one of seven women to be in the first group to go to fighter pilot school. When she graduated, Martha went to Kuwait in the Middle East. There, she participated in Operation Southern Watch. Their job was to keep Iraqi planes from flying in the United Nations' "no-fly zone."

Women soldiers had to wear sweat pants in desert countries while men could wear shorts. That didn't seem fair to Martha. It was so hot, but she did not want to make trouble. A general's wife heard Martha mention that women were getting too hot in their clothes, and she told her husband. He changed the rule.

When Martha was **deployed** to Saudi Arabia, she saw that things were worse for female soldiers. They had to wear **abayas** (Muslim robes), while the men could wear their regular uniforms. The women could not go off the base without a man to **chaperone** them. They weren't allowed to drive. They had to sit in the backseat. Martha thought these rules were wrong for many reasons.

TIDBITS

In 1993, Martha won the military division of an important triathlon. It was the Hawaii Ironman World Triathlon Championship. The race has a 26.2-mile run, 112-mile bike race, and a 2.4-mile ocean swim.

Martha was the first woman to command a fighter squadron.

How could soldiers be a strong group when some soldiers had to behave differently from the others? Why was she allowed to fly a plane but not to drive a car? How could a woman give orders to men who she'd have to sit behind? Why should some soldiers have to wear clothes that were part of a religion that wasn't theirs?

The military trains soldiers to take orders and not complain. Martha wondered how much trouble she would get in for trying to change the rules. She had to try to fix things, though. She sued the Secretary of Defense. Martha knew she was risking her entire career. In 2002, she won her case. Congress voted unanimously that women soldiers should not be forced to wear the abaya.

TIDBITS

Martha's military awards include the Defense Superior Service Medal and the Bronze Star. She also won six Air Medals for combat missions.

Martha moved to Germany in 2010 to become a professor.

Martha McSally became one of the first women selected for fighter pilot school when the Department of Defense changed its policy.

Timeline: Martha McSally

1966 ➤ Martha McSally is born in Warwick, Rhode Island. Her parents are Bernard and Eleanor. She is the youngest of 5 children.

1978 ➤ Martha's father Bernard dies of a heart attack.

1984 ➤ Martha graduates at the top of her class at St. Mary Academy - Bay View.

1988 ➤ She graduates from the U.S. Air Force Academy.

1990 ➤ Martha graduates from Harvard University's John F. Kennedy School of Government with a master's degree in public policy.

1991 ➤ Congress repeals the restriction against women becoming fighter pilots.

1993 ➤ The Department of Defense changes its policy on women as fighter pilots. Martha is selected for fighter pilot school.

1995 ➤ She is deployed to Kuwait. She begins asking her commanders to fix the policy about what clothes women soldiers have to wear.

1995–96 ➤ Martha does a tour of duty in Iraq for Operation Southern Watch.

2000 ➤ Martha is in Saudi Arabia, also for Operation Southern Watch.

2002 ➤ Martha wins a lawsuit about women soldiers having to wear abayas in Saudi Arabia.

2004 ➤ Martha takes command of the 354th Fighter Squadron at Davis-Monthan Air Force Base in Arizona. She is the first woman to command a fighter squadron. Her squadron goes to Afghanistan for Operation Enduring Freedom.

2005 ➤ Martha's squadron wins the Air Force Association's David C. Shilling Award, given for the best aerospace contribution to defense.

2006 ➤ Martha is promoted to full colonel.

2007 ➤ Martha graduates from Air War College, Air University with a Master's Degree in Strategic Studies. Air War College gives Martha their Leadership Award.

2010 ➤ Martha retires from active duty in the military. She becomes a Professor of National Security Studies with the George C. Marshall European Center for Security Studies in Germany.

2012 ➤ Martha McSally runs for Congress in Arizona but loses a close election.

Learn more about Martha McSally and Women in the Military

- Donelly, Karen. ***American Women Pilots of World War II.*** Rosen Classroom, 2009.
- Langley, Wanda. ***Flying Higher: The Women Airforce Service Pilots of World War II.*** Linnet Books, 2002.
- Schwartz, Heather. ***Women of the U.S. Air Force.*** Capstone Press, 2011.
- Zeinert, Karen and Mary Miller. ***The Brave Women of the Gulf Wars: Operation Desert Storm and Operation Iraqi Freedom.*** 21st Century, 2006.

Web sites:

- Air Force Lt. Col. Martha McSally discusses her career: http://www.defense.gov/home/faceofdefense/fod/2006-12/f20061207a.html

Glossary

abayas (uh BAY uhz) Loose-fitting, long black robes worn by some Muslim women that cover them from head to toe.

chaperone (SHAP uh ROHN) In this story, a man who accompanies a woman in public to protect her and to supervise her behavior.

deployed (di PLOID) Sent into battle.

public policy (PUHB lik POL uh see) In this story, the study of the laws, regulations, and actions put into force by a government.

—24—

Jill Craybas: Tennis Star, Olympic Athlete

By Barbara Keevil Parker

Jill wanted to be on the U.S. Olympic women's tennis team for the 2008 Beijing China Olympics. However, she was not selected.

On August 8th, her phone rang. The voice on the other end told her she had been chosen to replace one of the players who withdrew. Jill was delighted. She called her family to share the news. Jill had little time to make arrangements to fly to Beijing.

Jill Craybas was born July 4, 1974. She grew up in East Greenwich, Rhode Island.

Jill attended Lincoln School, an all girls' school, in Providence, Rhode Island. She earned **All-State** in tennis. The U.S. Tennis Association awarded her the National Sportsmanship Award.

From age 12 to 18, Jill played in **NELTA**, the New England section of tennis for juniors in the U.S. She became one of the top-10 junior tennis players in the United States. Before finishing high school, she won two major tournaments, one in Memphis and the Seventeen Tour of

Champions in Mission Viejo, California. These wins launched her career, raised her **rankings**, and brought her college scholarship offers.

Jill played college tennis for two years at the University of Texas. She suffered stress fractures, but helped her team win a national tennis championship.

She transferred to the University of Florida and became a star. Again, she helped her team to win a national championship in women's tennis. She became a tennis **All-American** and the school's Female Athlete of the Year. She was ranked the #1 women's singles player in the country. Jill graduated with a degree in **telecommunications**.

At age 21, Jill began playing **professional** tennis. She knew being 5-foot 3 inches tall put her at a disadvantage. She had to work hard to cover all corners of a tennis court. Players with longer legs could get to the tennis ball faster. However, her high energy made up for her height.

Since turning professional, Jill has played in major tennis tournaments around the world. One of her most exciting wins came at Wimbledon in 2005. Jill's opponent was Serena Williams. Serena was a two-time champion. Jill was an underdog. Jill shocked Serena and those watching the match. She won.

After winning, Jill said, "It feels great and I don't know if my achievement has truly sunk in. It's a big moment for me." The next day, Venus Williams, Serena's sister, defeated Jill.

By 2006, Jill had 39 singles wins.

TIDBITS

In 1970, nine women competed in a series of tennis matches. Philip Morris, a tobacco company, paid the prize money. They called it the Virginia Slims Series. The Series became the Women's Tennis Association (WTA) in 1973.

Jill helped the Universities of Texas and Florida win national championships. She is the only woman to play on two championship teams at two different colleges.

TIDBITS

The WTA awards tennis players points based on the tournaments they enter, and points for how far they advance in a tournament. The WTA adds up each player's points to determine a player's ranking. The player with the most points is ranked #1. The Olympic tennis team is selected based on rankings.

A highlight of 2008 was her trip to the Olympics as a member of the U.S. Women's Tennis Team. She played in the singles event. She didn't win a medal, but loved being there.

In 2010, Jill played at the U.S. Open in Flushing, New York. Humidity hovered in the air. The heat reached 96 to 110 degrees. Jill won the first set, but the heat and humidity made her sick. She played on. Her body cramped. During breaks, her trainers rubbed her arms and legs with ice. The officials asked if she needed to quit. She said, "I've never retired from a match in my life." She lost the match but she didn't quit.

In 2010, The Women's Tennis Association (WTA) ranked Jill Craybas in the top 100 players for the tenth year in a row.

Today, Jill lives in Huntington Beach, California.

Jill Crabas began her professional tennis career at age twenty-one.

Timeline: Jill Craybas

1974	July 4, Jill Craybas is born in Providence, RI, to Norbert and Camille Craybas.
1992	As an amateur, Jill Craybas plays her first International Tennis Federation **Circuit** in the junior division and is ranked #8.
1993	She helps the University of Texas win a national tennis title.
1995	Jill becomes University of Florida's Female Athlete of the Year.
1996	She becomes the **NCAA** Singles champion at the University of Florida.
	She is ranked the #1 women's singles player in the country.
	Jill graduates from the University of Florida.
	June, she turns professional, enters the U.S. Open, and makes a **Grand Slam debut.**
1997	Jill suffers a stress fracture and can't play.
1998	Jill tours and wins her first professional title at an ITF event.
2000	Jill qualifies for the Auckland, New Zealand Open and U.S. Open.
2001	For the first time she plays all four major tennis tournaments: Wimbledon, U.S. Open, French Open, and Australia Open.
	She wins her first Grand Slam match.
2002	She wins her first tour singles title at the Japan Open, becoming the oldest first-time winner. She is 28 years old.
2003	Jill wins her first Tour doubles title at Madrid, Spain.
2004	The World Tennis Association (WTA) women tennis players elect Jill to the WTA Tour Players' Council.
2004–2006	She becomes a member of US Federation Cup Team.
2005	The World Tennis Association ranks her in the top 50 players.
	She beats Serena Williams at Wimbledon, but loses to champion Venus Williams.
2006	April 17, she reaches a career-high of 39 singles wins.
2008	Jill plays in Beijing Olympics.
2010	For the tenth year in a row, Jill Craybas is ranked in the top 100 players.
	Lincoln School installs her in their Athlete Hall of Fame.

Learn More About Jill Craybas and Tennis

- Ditchfield, Christian. ***Tennis (True Books)***. Children's Press, 2003.
- Guillermo-Newton, Judith. ***Competitive Tennis for Girls (Sportsgirl)***. Rosen Publishing Group, 2001.
- Rusch, Elizabeth. ***Girls' Tennis: Conquering the Court (Girls Got Game)***. Capstone Press, 2007.

Web sites:

- An article about Jill Craybas making the Olympic team: http://news.providencejournal.com/sports/2008/08/east-greenwichs.html
- A short biography of Jill Craybas by the Lincoln School Hall of Fame: http://www.lincolnschool.org/page.cfm?p=1690

Glossary

All-American An athlete honored as one of the best amateurs in the U.S.

All-State Someone chosen to represent one's state in a competition.

circuit (SUR kit) A group of competitions.

debut (day BYOO) In this story, a first-time appearance in a sports competition.

Grand Slam Winning all the major competitions in a season especially in tennis or golf.

NCAA **N**ational **C**ollegiate **A**thletic **A**ssociation

NELTA **N**ew **E**ngland **L**awn **T**ennis **A**ssociation.

professional (pruh FESH uh nuhl) Making money for doing something others do for fun, as in a professional athlete.

rankings (RANGK ingz) An athlete's position in a list of players based on games played and won.

telecommunications (TEL uh kuh myoo nuh KAY shuhnz) The study of how messages are sent over the Internet, satellites, telephones, and other methods of electronic communication.

—25—

Elizabeth Beisel:

Olympic Swimmer

by Marcia Maynard

Eighteen year old Elizabeth waved to the crowd. She tucked her blond curly hair into her bathing cap. She stepped to the edge of the pool, put on her goggles and focused. She was competing at the **Pan Pacific Championships**. She faced seven of the best female swimmers in the world. They came from Australia, Canada, Japan and the U. S. It was going to be a difficult race.

. . . . ∾ . . . .

Elizabeth Beisel was born in Saunderstown, Rhode Island on August 18, 1992. Her father, Ted, is a construction superintendent. Her mother, Joan, worked for American Airlines for twenty five years. Elizabeth has one younger brother.

Swimming has always been part of Elizabeth's life. She started swim lessons before she even learned to walk. By the time she was ten, she joined the Bluefish **competitive** swim club in Attleboro, Massachusetts.

Elizabeth's mother drove her to practice after school each day. It took forty minutes to drive to the indoor pool and home again. Elizabeth didn't have much free time so she usually did her homework in the car. But Elizabeth never complained. She thought swimming was the best sport there was.

Elizabeth was in middle school when she started racing internationally. She was young, but she was quickly becoming one of the best female swimmers in the world.

In ninth grade Elizabeth joined her high school team. She still swam daily with her Bluefish club in Massachusetts. She dreamed of being in the Olympics.

That dream came true when she was only fifteen. She said, "It happened so fast. I always wanted to be an **Olympian**, but I definitely didn't think it would happen in 2008." In August, Elizabeth traveled to Beijing, China with the USA swim team for the summer Olympics. She was the youngest member of the team. She came in fourth in the **400 meter IM** and fifth in the **200 meter backstroke**. She just missed earning an Olympic medal.

Elizabeth turned sixteen the day she flew home from the Olympics. Her friends and family met her at the airport with balloons. Later on, they celebrated her birthday and her accomplishments.

Even though Elizabeth had become an Olympian, she continued swimming on her high school swim team. "These are my friends," Beisel said. She believed having an Olympic swimmer on the high school team would help high schoolers

TIDBITS

Elizabeth's last name is pronounced, Bye-zul.

Elizabeth started playing the violin when she was six. She was first chair All-State as a violinist when she was a high school **freshman**. She also plays piano, surfs and plays golf.

At age ten, Elizabeth set seven national records for her age group.

become excited about swimming.

In 2010, Elizabeth graduated from North Kingston High School. Later that summer, she was part of the Pan Pacific Championships. When the starting horn sounded Elizabeth dove into the water. She swam to one end of the pool, turned underwater and swam back. Her first lap was over but she was behind many swimmers. Elizabeth had three more laps to go. As she finished her second lap she took the lead. Other swimmers were close behind. Finally, Elizabeth finished her last lap. The race was finished. She looked up at the timer on the wall and smiled. She had won her first international gold medal.

Elizabeth now attends the University of Florida. She enjoys having a new swim coach and new swim team friends. As she keeps improving as a swimmer, she'll qualify for more races. Even though she had been in the 2008 Olympics, she had to qualify to be in the 2012 Olympics. She was fast enough to win her first Olympic medals.

Elizabeth Beisel was only fifteen when she became an Olympian.

TIDBITS

One of her major accomplishments in high school was learning how to handle pressure and nerves. As she continues swimming and competing, she's no longer nervous about making a team. Instead, she focuses on breaking records.

Elizabeth is the first Olympic swimmer from Rhode Island since 1964.

After Elizabeth qualified for the 2008 Olympics, a friend gave her an Olympic Barbie doll that had Olympic rings on the bathing suit.

Timeline: Elizabeth Beisel

1992 ➤ August 18, Elizabeth is born the first of two children to Ted and Joan Beisel, in Saunderstown, Rhode Island. She has a younger brother, Danny.

2002 ➤ Elizabeth starts competing for the Blue Fish Swim Club.

2005 ➤ She makes the Pan Pacific National Team.

She qualifies for World Championship in Melbourne, Australia.

2008 ➤ August, Elizabeth competes in Summer Olympics in Beijing, China.

She is the youngest member of the USA Beijing swim team.

August 18, Elizabeth celebrates her sixteenth birthday the same day she flies home from the 2008 Olympics.

2010 ➤ June, She graduates from North Kingstown High School, North Kingstown, RI.

August, Elizabeth wins her first and second international gold medals at the Pan Pacific swim meet.

August, She enters the University of Florida on a full athletic **scholarship.**

November, Elizabeth wins the Southeastern Conference Swimmer of the Week award for the third time. She is the first college freshman to win this award three times.

2011 ➤ July 30, Elizabeth wins a gold medal in the 400-meter individual medley at the FINA World Championships in Shanghai.

August 4, She wins the 400-meter individual medley at the ConocoPhillips U.S. swimming championships.

2012 ➤ June, Elizabeth qualifies for the London Summer Olympics during the trials held in Omaha, Nebraska.

August, she receives a silver medal in the 400 meter individual medley and a bronze medal in the 200 meter backstroke.

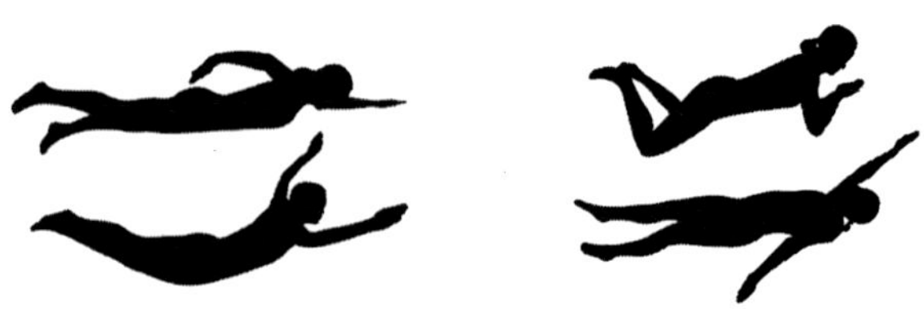

Learn More About Elizabeth Beisel and Swimming

- Macy, Sue. ***National Geographic Swifter, Higher, Stronger, a Photographic History of the Summer Olympics.*** National Geographic Society, 2008.
- Rouse, Jeff. ***The Young Swimmer, A Young Enthusiast's Guide to Swimming.*** DK publishing, 1997.
- Verrier, John. ***Successful Sports, Swimming.*** Rigby Interactive Library, 1997.

Web sites:

- Watch Elizabeth Beisil win the Pan Pacific Gold: http://www.youtube.com/watch?v = tzUs7X2ThhE
- Official website of the Olympic Games: http://www.olympic.org

Glossary

competitive (kuhm PET uh tiv) Always trying to win.

400 meter IM (individual medley) A race swum by one person who must complete four different styles of swimming: butterfly stroke, back stroke, breast stroke, and free-style.

freshman (FRESH muhn) The first year of high school or college.

Olympian (oh LIM pee uhn) An athlete who is chosen to compete in the Olympic Games.

Pan Pacific Championships A tough swimming competition that is held every four years. It began as a contest between countries who were not allowed to participate in the European Championships. It was originally open to countries who bordered the Pacific Ocean. Today, other countries (like Brazil) have been allowed to participate.

scholarship (SKOL ur ship) A gift of money that pays for someone to attend college or do a special course of study.

200 meter backstroke A swimming stroke performed on one's back, using over-arm strokes and a flutter kick. It is the only stroke in swimming competitions that starts in the water. The swimmer must do four, 50-meter laps (from one end of the pool to the other is a lap).

Research, Interviews, and Special Thanks

Additional research conducted at:

- Newport Historical Society
- Rhode Island Historical Society, Providence, RI
- Providence Public Libraries
- Rhode Island School of Design
- Brown University Libraries

Interviews conducted with:

- Claudine Schneider
- Janet Moreau

Special thanks to:

- Bert Lippincott, of the Newport Historical Society
- Phoebe Bean, of the Rhode Island Historical Society
- Ruth Buzzi for posts made on Twitter about her interests and life
- Nicole Chalfant, of the Prudence Crandall Museum
- Cam Craybas, Jill's mother, for reading the manuscript about her daughter
- Mark Kellner for allowing author Sally Riley to visit the Ida Lewis Yacht Club and see the lantern tower and the rooms in the house where Ida lived
- Jane Lancaster (Historian, Visiting Professor at Brown University)
- Adam McFarren, of the American Alpine Club Library, Golden, CO
- Janet Moreau for her time and willingness to be interviewed for this article, as well as her generosity of spirit
- Claudine Schneider for fact-checking the manuscript about her life
- Loren Spears, Director of the Tomaquag Indian Memorial Museum

A complete research bibliography for *Women of the Ocean State: 25 Rhode Island Women You Should Know* is available in a downloadable PDF format from Apprentice Shop Books, LLC at www.apprenticeshopbooks.com

*Partial Research Bibliography**

CHAPTER 1: Anne Hutchinson: *Co-founder of Rhode Island, Religious Activist*

Behling, Sam. "Anne Marbury Hutchinson." *RootsWeb Genealogical Data Cooperative.* N.p., n.d. Web. 09 Jan. 2011. < http://homepages.rootsweb.ancestry.com/ ~ sam/ marbury/anne.html >.

Kizer, Kay. *University of Notre Dame.* Rep. N.p., n.d. Web. 09 Jan. 2011. < http://www.nd.edu/ ~ rbarger/www7/ puritans.html >.

LaPlante, Eve. *American Jezebel: the Uncommon Life of Anne Hutchinson, the Woman Who Defied the Puritans.* [San Francisco]: HarperSanFrancisco, 2004. Print.

Leonardo, Bianca, and Winnifred King. Rugg. *Anne Hutchinson: Unsung Heroine of History.* Joshua Tree, CA: Tree of Life Publications, 1995. Print.

CHAPTER 2: Ann Smith Franklin: *Colonial Printer*

"About this Paper: The Newport Mercury," Library of Congress, Web. 05 Nov. 2010. < http://chroniclingamerica.loc.gov/ lccn/sn83021176/ >.

Albertine, Susan. *A Living of Words: American Women In Print Culture,* Knoxville: University of Tennessee Press, 1995. pp 1-17.

"Ann Smith Franklin," Columbia Electronic Encyclopedia, 6th Edition, p. 1-1, 1p. Web. 01 July 2010.

"Ann Smith Franklin," History of American Women Blog. Web. 05 Nov. 2010 < http://www.womenhistoryblog. com/2008/11/ann-smith-franklin.html >.

CHAPTER 3: Elleanor Eldridge: *Laborer and Businesswoman*

Davis, Karen. "Elleanor Eldridge: Entrepreneurial Pioneer." *Projo.com | The Providence Journal | Digital Extra.* The Providence Journal, 20 Feb. 1997. Web. 5 Feb. 2011. < http://www.projo.com/cgi-bin/include.pl/specials/ women/220bhs3.htm >.

"Elleanor Eldridge Biography – Entrepreneur, Tradeswoman « Maxizip.com." *Maxizip.com.* 29 Nov. 2010. Web. 10 May 2011. < http://maxizip.com/2010/11/elleanor-eldridge-biography-entrepreneur-tradeswoman/ >.

"Elleanor Eldridge, Businesswoman amid Oppression! | African American Registry." *The Black Box | African American Registry.* Web. 10 May 2011. < http://www. aaregistry.org/historic_events/view/elleanor-eldridge-businesswoman-amid-oppression >.

Fisher, Vivian Njeri. "Eldridge, Elleanor." *Black Women in America.* Ed. Darlene Clark. Hine. Oxford: Oxford UP, 2005. Print.

CHAPTER 4: Prudence Crandall: *Fighter for Equal Rights to Education*

"A Canterbury Tale: A Document Package for Connecticut's Prudence Crandall Affair," The Gilder/Lehrman Center for the Study of Slavery, Resistance, and Abolition, Yale Center for International and Area Studies. Web < http:// www.yale.edu/glc/crandall/index.htm >.

McCain, Diana Ross. *To All on Equal Terms,* Connecticut: Connecticut Commission on Arts, Tourism, Culture, History and Film, 2004.

Welch, Marvis Olive. *Prudence Crandall: A Biography.* Manchester, CT: Jason Publishers, 1983.

CHAPTER 5: Frances Harriet Whipple Green McDougall: *Writer for Those in Need*

Conley, Dr. Patrick T. *The Dorr Rebellion: Rhode Island's Crisis in Constitutional Government,* Providence: Rhode Island Bicentennial Foundation, 1976.

Deveny, John Patrick. *Paschal Beverly Randolph: a nineteenth-century Black American spiritualist,* Albany: State University of New York Press, 1997. Web. < http://tiny. cc/0jqi3 >.

"The First American Civil War: Glocester Remembers the Dorr Rebellion," *Rhode Island Roads. Web.* < http:// riroads.com/history/dorr_rebellion.htm >

"Frances Harriet Whipple Green McDougall." Web. < http:// faculty.ccri.edu/rprisco/RIWA/riwomenspeak/bookscans/ frances_harriet_whipple_green_mcdougall.html >.

CHAPTER 6: Elizabeth Buffam Chace: *Activist and Reformer*

Chace, Elizabeth Buffam, *Anti-slavery Reminiscences,* E. L Freeman and Sons, 1891

"Eliabeth Buffam Chace Family Papers." *Rhode Island Historical Society.* Web. 15 Nov. 2010. < http://www.rihs.org/mssinv/ Mss1002.htm >.

National Underground Railroad Freedom Center - Cincinnati, Ohio. Web. 15 Nov. 2010. < http://freedomcenter.org/ >.

Stevens, Elizabeth C. "Elizabeth Buffam Chace and Lillie Chace Wyman." *Rhode Island Monthly: Best of Rhode Island.* Web. 15 Nov. 2010. < http://www.quahog.org/factsfolklore/ index.php?id = 104 >.

The Religious Society of Friends. Web. 15 Nov. 2010. < http:// www.quaker.org >.

CHAPTER 7: Christiana Carteaux Bannister: *Black Businesswoman and Community Activist*

"10-R143." *The State of Rhode Island General Assembly.* Web. 2011. < http://www.rilin.state.ri.us/PublicLaws/law10/ res10/res10143.htm >.

Bannister, Christiana Carteaux. Boston, Oct. 11, 1864. Boston: Colored Ladies Commission of Boston, 1864. Print.

* A complete research bibliography is available in downloadable PDF format from www.apprenticeshopbooks.com

*continued Partial Research Bibliography**

Bannister House, Inc. Web. 2011. < http://bannisterhouse.org/history.htm >.

Blatt, Martin H., Thomas J. Brown, and Donald Yacovone. *Hope & Glory: Essays on the Legacy of the Fifty-Fourth Massachusetts Regiment.* Print.

Brown, William Wells. "Edward M. Bannister." The Black Man: His Antecedents, His Genius, and His Achievements. Boston: Thomas Hamilton, 1863. Print.

CHAPTER 8: Julia Ward Howe: *Poet and Reformer*

Cliffe, Peter. "'Battle Hymn' Author, Husband Fight a Long Battle Called Marriage." *The Washington Times* 4 Nov. 2000: 3. *Questia Online Library.* Web. 10 May 2011. < http://www.questia.com/reader/printPaginator/167 >.

Clifford, Deborah Pickman. *Mine Eyes Have Seen the Glory: A Biography of Julia Ward Howe.* Boston: Little, Brown, 1979. Print.

Howe, Julia W. *Reminiscences 1819-1899.* Boston: Houghton Mifflin, 1899. *Questia Online Library.* Web. 11 May 2011. < http://www.questia.com/PM.qst?a = o&d = 55373708 >.

Huxman, Susan S. "Julia Ward Howe (1819-1910), Patriotic Crusader for Woman's Rights and Peace." *Women Public Speakers in the United States, 1800-1925: A Bio-Critical Sourcebook.* Westport, CT: Greenwood, 1993. 434-47. *Questia Online Library.* Web. 10 May 2011. < http://www.questia.com/reader/printPaginator/174 >.

CHAPTER 9: Sarah Elizabeth Doyle: *Champion for Women's Education*

Barrett, Dawn, and Andrew Martinez. Infinite Radius: Founding Rhode Island School of Design. Providence: Rhode Island School of Design, 2008. Print.

Doyle, Sarah E. "Programme of Work for Members, Seventeenth Annual Report, March 1, 1893." History of the Rhode Island Women's Club 1876-1893. Print.

"Encyclopedia Brunoniana | Pembroke Hall." Brown University. Web. Jan. 2011. < http://www.brown.edu/Administration/News_Bureau/Databases/Encyclopedia/search.php?serial = P0110 >.

McPhillips, Jody. "Projo.com's THE RHODE ISLAND CENTURY Special, Month One: Founding Mothers." January 24, 1999. Rhode Island, Providence, | Projo.com | The Providence Journal. Web. Jan. 2011.

CHAPTER 10: Ida Lewis: *Lighthouse Keeper, American Heroine*

Anderson, Kraig. "Ida Lewis Rock Lighthouse, Rhode Island at Lighthousefriends.com." *Lighthouse Friends.* Lighthouse Friends. Web. 02 May 2011. < http://www.lighthousefriends.com/light.asp?ID = 398 >.

D'Entremont, Jeremy. "Lime Rock Lighthouse (Ida Lewis Yacht Club) History." *New England Lighthouses: A Virtual Guide - Photos,history, Tours, Cruises, Coastal Accommodations and More.* New England Lighthouses: A Virtual Guide, 21 Jan. 2007. Web. 02 May 2011. < http://lighthouse.cc/limerock/history.html >.

Haley, John W. "Ida Lewis." *Quahog.org Facts and Folklore Ida Lewis.* Quahog.org, 24 Nov. 2009. Web. 02 May 2011. < http://www.quahog.org/factsfolklore/index.php?id = 176 >.

CHAPTER 11: Annie Smith Peck: *Mountain Climber*

"Annie Smith Peck | Biographies." *Frauen-BiographieForschung | Fembio.org.* Web. 11 Feb. 2011. < http://www.fembio.org/english/biography.php/woman/biography/annie-smith-peck/ >.

"Annie Smith Peck Biography." *Biography.com.* Web. 11 Feb. 2011. < http://www.biography.com/articles/Annie-Smith-Peck-215064 >.

"Annie Smith Peck Summary | BookRags.com." *BookRags.com | Study Guides, Lesson Plans, Book Summaries and More.* Web. 11 Feb. 2011. < http://www.bookrags.com/research/annie-smith-peck-ued/ >.

"Girl Who Risked Life To Climb Mountain, Now To Fly Over It." *Meriden Record.* Oct. 21, 1929. Web. *Google News.* 11 Feb. 2011. < http://news.google.com/newspapers?id = nl1HAAAAIBAJ&sjid = xf4MAAAAIBAJ&pg = 6356,4106909&dq = annie smith peck timeline&hl = en >.

CHAPTER 12: Alva Vanderbilt Belmont: *Socialite and Suffragette*

"Alva Ertskin Smith Vanderbilt Belmont." *Dictionary of American Biography.* New York: Charles Scribner's Sons, 1944. *Gale Biography in Context.* Web. 25 Oct. 2010.

Buell, Janet W. "Alva Belmont: from Socialite to Feminist." *Historian* 52.2 (1990): 219. *Academic Search Premier.* EBSCO. Web. 19 Nov. 2010.

"The Gilded Age." *Digital History.* Web. 04 Feb. 2011. < http://www.digitalhistory.uh.edu/modules/gilded_age/index.cfm >.

Kahn, Eve M. "The Stuff She Collected, Gilded and Not." *New York Times* 7 May 2010: C29(L). *Gale Biography in Context.* Web. 25 Oct. 2010.

CHAPTER 13: Matilda Sissieretta Joyner Jones: *Opera Singer*

Foster, Catherine D. "Jones, Sissieretta (1869-1933) | The Black Past: Remembered and Reclaimed." | The Black Past: Remembered and Reclaimed. The Black Past. Web. 12 Dec. 2010. < http://www.blackpast.org/?q = aah/jones-sissieretta-1869-1933 >.

Kalfatovic, Mary. "Matilda Sissieretta Joyner." Encyclopedia.com. Web. 12 Dec. 2010. < http://www.encyclopedia.com/topics/M._Sissieretta_Jones.aspx >

*continued Partial Research Bibliography**

Liberman, Ellen. "Sissieretta Jones: A Voice of Great Richness." Rhode Island, Providence, News, Sports, Entertainment, Ads | Projo.com | The Providence Journal. *Providence Journal.* Web. 12 Dec. 2010. < http://www.projo.com/cgi-bin/include.pl/specials/women/220bhs1.htm >.

"Sissieretta Jones." Black History Pages. Web. 12 Dec. 2010. < http://www.blackhistorypages.net/pages/sjones.php >

CHAPTER 14: Nancy Elizabeth Prophet: *African-American Sculptor*

Amaki, Amalia. "The Unfulfilled Promise of Nancy Elizabeth Prophet." *The International Review of African American Art* 18.3 (2002): 23-31. Print.

Amaki, Amalia K., and Andrea Barnwell. Brownlee. *Hale Woodruff, Nancy Elizabeth Prophet,and the Academy.* Atlanta: Spelman College Museum of Fine Art, 2007. Print.

Brown University Library, Center for Digital Initiatives. Web. 06 Jan. 2011. < http://dl.lib.brown.edu/repository2/repoman.php?verb = render&id = 1206038647140625 >.

Duncan, Michael. "Freeing the Figure." *Art in America* (April 1996): 44-47. Print.

CHAPTER 15: Princess Red Wing: *Speaker for Her Tribe*

Bomster, Mark. "A Native Daughter, Princess Redwing of the Narragansetts," *The Good 5¢ Cigar*, April 12, 1976.

Cech, John "Princess Red Wing: Keeper of the Past," *Children's Literature,* vol. 10, 1982, pp. 83-101.

Cech, John. "Princess Red Wing, Many Reasons, Many Thanksgivings," *The Christian Science Monitor,* November 26, 1980.

"D.A.R. Women Hear Princess Describe Indian Folk Lore," *The Woonsocket Call,* November 19, 1940.

CHAPTER 16: Janet Moreau Stone: *Olympic Gold Medal Runner*

Donaldson, Jim. "Rhode Island's first gold medalist to shine spiritual light on Olympians," 4 Aug. 4, 2008. < http://www.projo.com/sports/jimdonaldson/sp_oly_jim_donaldson04_08-04-08_1IB2AM7_v13.3e8610e.html >

Interview with Janet Moreau and the author, February 12, 2011.

CHAPTER 17: Jacqueline Kennedy Onassis: *First Lady of the United States*

1961, March. "Jackie Kennedy Biography :: National First Ladies' Library." *National First Ladies' Library.* Web. 01 Mar. 2011. < http://www.firstladies.org/biographies/firstladies.aspx?biography = 36 >.

Bradford, Sarah. *America's Queen: the Life of Jacqueline Kennedy Onassis.* New York: Viking, 2000. Print.

"Jacqueline Lee Bouvier Kennedy." *The White House.* Web. 01 Mar. 2011. < http://www.whitehouse.gov/about/first-ladies/jacquelinekennedy >.

"Life of Jacqueline B. Kennedy - John F. Kennedy Presidential Library & Museum." *John F. Kennedy Presidential Library & Museum.* Web. 01 Apr. 2011. < http://www.jfklibrary.org/JFK/Life-of-Jacqueline-B-Kennedy.aspx >.

CHAPTER 18: Ruth Buzzi: *Actor and Comedian*

Olson, James S. (edited), *Historical Dictionary of the 1960s,* Greenwood Press, Westport, Connecticut-London, 1999.

Twitter. Web. Jan. through May 2011. < http://twitter.com/ >.

"Ruth Buzzi Biography." *Movie Tickets & Movie Times - Fandango.com.* Web. 20 Apr. 2011. < http://www.fandango.com/ruthbuzzi/biography/p9987 >.

"Ruth Buzzi." *Web Hosting Using Many Tools ColdFusion FrontPage and More.* Web. 25 Apr. 2011. < http://www.webpan.com/thelaughin/tips04.htm >.

CHAPTER 19: Jennifer Murray: *Record Breaking Helicopter Pilot*

Drew, Emma. "Flying to Extremes: Polar First." Web. 18 July 2011. < http://www.polarfirst.com >.

Extreme world record breaking helicopter Journey : 171-day, 32,206-nautical-mile pole-to-pole trip. :23 May, 2007 Web. 18 July 2011. < http://www.engineerdir.com/press/catalog/1253/ >.

"Helicopter Pilots Try Pole-to-pole Trip - Technology & Science - Science - Msnbc.com." Msnbc.com - Breaking News, Science and Tech News, World News, US News, Local News- Msnbc.com. Web. 18 July 2011. < http://www.msnbc.msn.com/id/16065818/ns/technology_and_science-science/t/helicopter-pilots-attempt-pole-to-pole-journey/ >.

"Helicopter Pilots Finish Record Pole-To-Pole Trip — MercoPress." *News from Latin America and Mercosur — MercoPress.* Web. 18 July 2011. < http://en.mercopress.com/2007/05/25/helicopter-pilots-finish-record-pole-to-pole-trip >.

CHAPTER 20: Joyce Jillson: *Actress, Author, Astrologer*

Back Stage. 45th ed. Vol. 45. OBITUARIES. *Business Source Premier.* Web. 5 Nov. 2004.

Bacon, Doris Klein. "Real Women Don't Pump Gas, But Joyce Jillson Gets Top Mileage from Her Quickie Spin-Off Book." Web. < http://www.people.com/people/archive/article/0,,20084836,00.html >.

Cook, Michael. "Joyce Jillson Astrologer to the Stars: Bridging the Gap between Serious Astrology and Entertainment Astrology." Mercator, 18 Nov. 2004. Web. < http://www.

* A complete research bibliography is available in downloadable PDF format from www.apprenticeshopbooks.com

continued Partial Research Bibliography *

mercatornet.com/articles/view/joyce_jillson_astrologer_to the_stars/ >.

"Good Heavens! An Astrologer Dictating the President's Schedule? - TIME." *Breaking News, Analysis, Politics, Blogs, News Photos, Video, Tech Reviews - TIME.com.* 16 May 1988. Web. < http://www.time.com/time/magazine/article/0,9171,967389-1,00.html >.

CHAPTER 21: Claudine Schneider: *Congresswoman and Environmental Leader*

"100% Vote Citizen Action News," *Social Policy,* Winter 1990, vol. 20, issue 3, p. 43-5.

Bolding, Keri. "Former U.S. Congresswoman Claudine Schneider is back on the Campaign Trail in Rhode Island" e-wire, Center for Resource Solutions. 2/18/2002. Web. 06 April 2011. < http://www.ewire.com/display.cfm/Wire_ID/1501 >.

"Claudine Schneider," *Biographical Directory of the United States Congress.* Web. 06 April 2011. < http://bioguide.congress.gov/scripts/biodisplay.pl?index = S000136 >

"Claudine Schneider," Claudine Schneider web site. Web. 06 April 2011.Web. 06 April 2011. < www.claudineschneider.com >.

CHAPTER 22: Ojetta Rogeriee Thompson: *A Judge for Changing Times*

Alongi, Paul. "Sterling High School Greenville, South Carolina History." South Carolina SC - Genealogical and Historical Websites. Web. 15 Mar. 2011. < http://sciway3.net/greenville-historical-schools/SCIwaySterling.htm >.

"Arent Fox LLP: FTC Wins Big in Case about Deceptive Infomercials." Arent Fox LLP: Practicing Law Since 1942, with Offices in Washington, DC, New York City and Los Angeles. 11 Nov. 2010. Web. 15 Mar. 2011. < http://www.arentfox.com/publications/index.cfm?fa = legalUpdateDisp&content_id = 2799 >.

"Biographical Directory of Federal Judges: Thompson, Ojetta Rogeriee." www.fjc.gov. Federal Judicial Center. Web. 15 Mar. 2011. < http://www.fjc.gov/servlet/nGetInfo?jid = 3233&cid = 999&ctype = na&instate = na >.

Clifton, Reza Corinne. "Ink-filled Water Guns and Summers in Tennessee." The Providence American Newspaper 23 Mar. 2006. Print.

CHAPTER 23: Martha McSally: *Warrior Pilot*

Bergquist, Carl. "Air Force Lt. Col. Martha McSally: First female pilot in combat reflects on career." *United States Department of Defense.* 06 Dec. 2006. Web. 07 July 2011. < http://www.defense.gov/home/faceofdefense/fod/2006-12/f20061207a.html >.

Gerhart, Ann. "Martha McSally's Garb In Saudi Arabia Chafed, So She Pressed a Lawsuit." *Washington Post.* 07 Jan. 2002.

"McSally, Martha." *The Marshall Center.* Web. 07 July 2011. < http://www.marshallcenter.org/mcpublicweb/en/component/content/article/863-mcsally-martha.html?directory = 30 >.

McSally, Martha. "Women in combat: is the current policy obsolete?" *Duke Journal of Gender Law & Policy.* 16 Jul. 2007.

CHAPTER 24: Jill Craybas: *Tennis Star, Olympic Athlete*

About the WTA: *The WTA Story.* Web. 31 Aug. 2010. < http://www.wtatennis.com/page/AboutTheTour/0,,12781,00.html >.

American Female Tennis Players: Rosemary Casals, Tracy Austin, Jill Craybas, Nicole Arendt, Mary Carillo, Audra Cohen, Anne White. LLC, 2010. Print.

Chadband, Ian, and Raoul Simons. "Venus Avenges Sister's Defeat and Crushes Jill." *The Evening Standard* 27 June 2005: 1. Print.

Cheyne, George. "Tennis:Wimbledon 2005: Tears As Jill-ted Serena Crashes." *Sunday Mail: Scottish Daily Record and Sunday* 26 June 2005: 80. Print.

CHAPTER 25: Elizabeth Beisel: *Olympic Swimmer*

Devaney, Jason. "News | U.S. Swimmer Beisel Finds Success at Young Age | Universal Sports." *Year-Round Coverage of Olympic Sports & Athletes | Universal Sports.* 07 Dec. 2009. Web. 29 Jan. 2011. < http://www.universalsports.com/news/article/newsid = 375472.html >.

Edgar, Randal. "Hundreds Will Join Beisel's Dad in Watching Olympics on TV | North Kingstown | Projo.com | The Providence Journal." *Rhode Island, Providence, News, Sports, Entertainment, Ads | Projo.com | The Providence Journal.* 08 Aug. 2008. Web. 29 Jan. 2011. < http://www.projo.com/ri/northkingstown/content/BEISEL_FUNDRAISER_08-08-08_PHB53FU_v112.4040bd9.html >.

Fleming, Arline A. "Bound for Beijing - Dedication Earns Beisel an Olympic Berth | North Kingstown | Projo.com | The Providence Journal." *Rhode Island, Providence, News, Sports, Entertainment, Ads | Projo.com | The Providence Journal.* 16 July 2008. Web. 29 Jan. 2011. < http://www.projo.com/ri/northkingstown/content/sc_swimmer_07-09-08_USAPAPI_v78.4041b95.html >.

Fleming, Arline A. "Teen Making a Splash in Swimming and Music." *Rhode Island, Providence, News, Sports, Entertainment, Ads | Projo.com | The Providence Journal.* 21 Dec. 2006. Web. 29 Jan. 2011. < http://www.projo.com/ri/northkingstown/content/sc_swim21_12-21-06_593BFND.2fbef59.html >.

* A complete research bibliography is available in downloadable PDF format from www.apprenticeshopbooks.com